D0984017

cesPrisonVoicesPrisonVoicesPrisonVoicesPrisonVo

nVoicesPrisonVoid

Voices

VoicesP

EDITED BY **Lee Weinstein and Richard Jaccoma**
PHOTOGRAPHY BY **Richard Jaccoma**

PrisonVoices

The John Howard Society of Canada

Library and Archives Canada Cataloguing in Publication

Prison voices / edited by Lee Weinstein and Richard Jaccoma;
photography by Richard Jaccoma.

ISBN 0-9689335-4-8

        1. Prisoners' writings, Canadian (English) 2. Canadian literature
(English)--21st century. 3. Prisoners--Canada--Literary collections. 4.
Prisoners--Canada--Biography. I. Weinstein, Lee II. Jaccoma, Richard
III. John Howard Society of Canada

PS8235.P7P75 2005   C810.8'09206927   C2005-904223-0

Editors: Lee Weinstein and Richard Jaccoma
Photographer: Richard Jaccoma
Designer: Shimizu Teryuki
Copy editor: Barbara Kuhne

John Howard Society of Canada
809 Blackburn Mews
Kingston, ON K7P 2N6
Telephone: 613-384-6272
Fax: 613-384-1847
Email: national@johnhoward.ca

Printed in Canada

Dedication

To the teachers, inmates, and former inmates of the Canadian correctional system.

Acknowledgements

We thank all the authors who shared their lives and their struggles with such great generosity.

Prison Voices was funded through a grant from the National Literacy Secretariat, Human Resources and Skills Development Canada. We are deeply grateful for their confidence in the project.

The unwavering support and understanding of Graham Stewart and the John Howard Society of Canada were absolutely essential to the creation of this book.

Prison Voices would not exist without the help of Karen Barclay, acting manager, Education and Personal Development Programs, Reintegration Programs, Correctional Service Canada. We extend our thanks to her and to Denis Barbe, acting director, Reintegration Programs, Correctional Service Canada.

Roy Glaremin and Rosie Rowbotham unlocked many doors.

Sandy Ward was an inspiration from start to finish. She added dimension to the concept, encouraged our work, and led our design team.

Our chief designer, Shimizu Teryuki, and his collaborator, Kaori Umezawa, laboured tirelessly, created brilliantly.

Ed Griffin deserves special thanks both for the fine writers he sent to us and for the inspiration he gives to students and colleagues.

One basic job of any editor is to separate good writing from less-good writing. In addition to that task we had a far more painful challenge: Selecting the top-quality writing we would publish, from the top-quality writing we needed to leave behind. We admit with dismay that there is another *Prison Voices* on the cutting-room floor. In that regard, we extend our special gratitude and apologies to three superior writers who made the final cut ... but were then left behind purely for reasons of space: Stephen Miles, Sandy Plante, and Jermaine Oshane Wilson.

Thanks to our highly skilled editorial team: Barbara Kuhne, Linnea Svahn-Jaccoma, and Carolyn McDonald. Thanks as well to Margaret Foster, Diane Genovese, Mary Lou Howarth, Janet Isserlis, Linda London, Barbara Moore, Elin Svahn, Mark McCue, and Max Weinstein; and to Dr. Barbara Burnaby for her guidance early in the process. We appreciate the continuing support and encouragement of Robert Chadwick, associate superintendent of School District #36, Surrey, British Columbia.

Table of Contents

Justice and Judgement
roxanne

Justice
and
Judgement

Justice and judgement often lie worlds apart.

Rape. It is the only crime where the victim becomes the accused.

Revenge. I forgot who I was, blinded by black happiness. I couldn't hear myself,
my heart and my mind weren't communicating. That was the tragedy.

To be in prison is no disgrace, I see both justice and injustice in the crime I committed. It is better
for me to be in a jail where I could bang the walls than in a jail I could not see. The end of who I
was began in prison.

In the beginning I went through periods of numbness that were harder to bear than grief. I can recall
standing in the shower with a razor to my wrist wanting so badly to die. I had never felt such hate
for my family like I did that day. I hated them for loving me so much; I couldn't do it and I knew it.

So here I sit listening to yet another program facilitator preach the same commonsense nonsense.
I have heard it so many times, the same answers to the same questions — it's almost insulting. I
look across the room and sense the atmosphere; it is caked with feeble hope. I watch my fellow
inmates' eyes light bright with plans for a better future — a clean future.

Graduation Day, another certificate meant to better us. Into the real world these so-called cured
women go; life's poisons/remedies take over. Addictions blind the willingly weak. Within weeks
they are back in prison. Looks like more premature resolutions failed, she's back reloaded with new
tales of drunken drugged adventures. That is the harsh reality I have become so aware of and hate.

Hate. I have come to the realization that all that I hate in others I hate in myself.

Courage. Tomorrow could bring change — will I grab it?

Lost Little Girl

Remembering the little girl I was growing up is like having a boulder placed on my chest. The person I am now cries, wishing to be that little girl again.

I was carefree and loving, I trusted people and accepted help when I needed it — anything and everything was possible. These days I feel nothing but regret and worry; I can't trust anyone and giving and receiving love is a struggle.

I often lie and think about my short life; I scrutinize every memory over and over again trying to find the exact moment and place that little girl left me.

When I was a child I would lie beside my mom and we would talk. We knew each other. When I got into drugs and alcohol, my mom and I became strangers.

I remember coming home one night — I walked in the house drunk and a mess. My mom starts yelling, asking where I was — telling me I can't go out anymore. I flip out and start crying uncontrollably; her eyes are panic and fear when she sees my tears.

I run out the door and walk down the street battling that little girl within me. She wants to run back home and tell mom she was raped, to cry in her arms and feel that safety again. I didn't let her. I was ashamed, I blamed myself, I felt dirty and like a whore — whatever that feels like. I washed the rape out of my life with soap and water. And I kept it out as long as I could with drugs and alcohol.

Looking back seems to get harder with knowledge. I have been clean for years and I am still searching for that little girl.

INTERVIEW: ROXANNE STEVENSON

QUESTION: Your home is so far away. Do you get many visitors here?
STEVENSON: Yes. I have cousins right around here.

Q: Does your mom come to visit?
S: Not since I've been here, no.

[She reads "In Her Eyes," the poem about her grandmother. Afterwards, she says this about the poem:]

S: That's at the lake, because Duck Bay's surrounded by lake on three sides.

Q: Is your grandmother still alive?
S: Yes.

Q: Have you ever read her the poem?
S: No. I never read it ... I never sent it to her. [Pause.] She was the oldest of thirteen kids. This is way back. So she had to raise them, had to work at a hotel for a dollar a day.

Q: How long ago?
S: How long? She's seventy-some now. Started working when she was nine. Had a hard life. And she's the smartest person I know.

Q: Smart how?
S: Just the things she'll say. Like I remember me and my brother used to fight. She always spoke straight Saulteaux [First Nations language, pronounced "Soto"]. She'd speak straight Saulteaux. And it would be like,

"You've got to love him, you know? What's going to happen?" Because I'd be like, "I hate him!" I would hate him; I don't anymore. She'd say you're going to, how you'd say in English, regret it.

Q: What's your grandmother like as a person?
S: Kind. A worrier. I think I'll be like her most likely when I grow older. She worries. She's always taking care of everybody.

Q: Are you a worrier now?
S: Sometimes. But in here it's kind of pointless.

Q: What was it like for you growing up?
S: It was good. I had a really good childhood.

Q: What's Duck Bay like?
S: It's small, and pretty much everybody's related to everybody. It's a really good place to grow up. Everyone speaks Saulteaux. I lived with my Koko, my Grandma; me and my mom. … Then we got our own place. Duck Bay was really good but we had to move away because it only went up to Grade 9, and I would have had to go away to Cranberry, and I didn't want to leave home. So we moved to Dauphin for high school.

Q: You describe a time of "trust and love" at home. When did that change for you?

S: When I stopped talking to my mom. It was probably the time I started getting high. It WAS the time I started getting high. I started doing drugs. I couldn't even ... I wouldn't talk to her anymore.

Q: What drugs were you doing?

S: I started off doing pot, then oil hash and 'shrooms. Never crack or needles. Because you don't see that much around Dauphin.

Q: In "Justice and Judgement" you use the term, a jail that you could not see. And you compare this jail you're in now, with the jail you could not see. What was the jail that you couldn't see?

S: The jail was ... after I was raped, I'd see him around, and I'd run and hide. I was ashamed and ... that was a jail.

Q: You say in "Justice and Judgement" that you sit in the various kinds of counselling programs and listen to the "commonsense nonsense." What do you mean by that?

S: I mean it's the same thing, every program, different titles, but the same thing, every program. Same reading out of the book, it's just useless to even answer questions because you already know it ... FLIP, Family Life Improvement Program ... OSAP, Offender Substance Abuse Program ... anger management, trauma and abuse. ... All these programs are exactly the same.

Q: Having been here awhile, you say that you've seen women go through the programs. ...

S: And come back ... leave ... or get into the spiritual and preach and preach and preach. You know. Something new comes in, they're right there.

Q: What kind of stuff?

S: You know, like Aboriginal ... the sweats ... the smudging ... following the Red Road-type talk. I've seen it.

Q: Did you grow up with a lot of spirituality in your home?

S: Yes. My grandma, my great-grandma.

Q: People you love.

S: Yes.

Q: Are you saying there's a problem with the spiritual?

S: Oh no ... with the people in programs. They go from programs to the spiritual to programs. Like we'll sit in programs and discuss things like, Why do you want to be clean? "For my kids." And I'll hear it and it's a bunch of lies because I'll see next night they're right there getting high. Or they leave, and they're back. Everybody comes back. Since I've been here, everybody has come back.

Q: And then there are people who feel that they were completely innocent and that nothing like this should have happened. Sounds like you're some-place in the middle.

S: Well, I'm guilty. And no, I don't think jail saved me.

Q: If you got out today, would you be afraid of re-offending in some way?

S: No. I'd be panicking, just to see people, even to see my own family.

Q: You say your mom hasn't been here. Is it just because of the distance?

S: [Nods.] Because of the distance.

Q: Does she write to you?

S: Yeah. Phone.

Q: Do you feel that you're close to her?

S: Yes. We've talked a lot since I've been in jail. ... I had to come to jail to get to know her again. ▣

Scars and Fire

Scars and fire
unhealed cries caged in
I am here and I hate me again.

I can't dig deep and save myself
I can't ask for help
I can't trust myself therefore I
cannot trust others.

Scars and fire
taking a son from a mother
the unbearable grief eats at me
my breath stops with every thought.

I see myself lying dead
bleeding from the wrists
the hurt has stopped — I'm done here
— no more pretending.

My spirit screams for help
but no one is coming — I'm alone

I am sick of waiting
to break, who do I tell?
I am here and I hate me again.

Alone, where I am supposed to be
where I deserve to be
in a darkness my hands are soggy with blood
his and mine
I'm done — shut off the tears and breathe.

In Her Eyes

In her eyes I find wisdom and truth.
She will always be here captured by this moment.
this moment nurtured by my soul.

The sun glistens over the gloriously flowing water.
Ducks and Geese fly free all around us.
A soft breeze brushes our skin and blows our hair.

I turn and tell her I love her without speaking.
She smiles and I know that she heard me.

In her eyes I see happiness and love.
She will always need me like I need her.
She lives in my heart, I live in hers.

for my Koko (Grandma) Myrtle

Prison Ain't Much of a Place

myles bolton

Prison is a place: where the first prisoner you see looks like an All-Canadian College boy, and you're surprised. Later you're disgusted because people on the outside still have the same prejudices that you used to have.

Prison is a place: where you write letters but can't think of anything to say.   Gradually you write fewer and fewer letters then finally stop altogether.

Prison is a place: where the flame in every man burns low. For some it flickers weakly, flashing brightly every once in a while but just never seems to burn as it once did before.

Prison is a place: where you hate through clenched teeth, where you want to beat, kick and punch. Then wonder if the psychologists know what they're talking about when they say you hate yourself.

Prison is a place: where you learn that not one person on this miserable planet needs You.

Prison is a place: where one can go for years at a time without the touch of a human hand; it may even be several months without hearing a kind word laced with love or affection.

It's a place where all your friendships are shallow and you know it.

Prison is a place: where you hear about a friend's divorce and can't recall if you even knew he was married.

Prison is a place: where you wait on a promised visit; when it doesn't come you worry endlessly about an accident.

Then when you find out the real reason why they never came, you're glad it wasn't serious. But you're bitter 'cause such a small thing kept them from coming to see you.

Prison is a place: where you see men that you respect, then you start to wonder if you like them or not.

It's a place where one strives to remain civilized, but as you lose your footing you do nothing but watch.

Prison is a place: where if you're married, you watch your marriage die.

It's a place where you learn that absence does not make the heart grow fonder but blacker. And you stop blaming your woman for wanting a real live man, instead of just a fading memory of one. I know that prison is a place where you go to bed before you're tired, then pull the blankets over your head even when you're not cold.

Gone But Not Forgotten

I'm drowning here and all you're doing

Is describing the water for me.

You left without even saying goodbye.

I miss your smile, your laugh,

And most of all

When you bite your lip

With a slight twinkle in your eye.

The first time around

Wasn't really all that bad,

Doing what I could to get over you.

I was never really that mad.

Then unexpectedly you had returned,

I felt a love that had been renewed,

Only to have that thrown out.

I'm back to where I was

When all of this began,

Older, Wiser, Smarter but sad.

I must say that I'm angry

At how you chose to leave,

But one thing that you have to know.

I love you and I'll never be mad.

Closure

There's an aching in my heart,

With a pounding in my head.

I'm so restless; it's hard to sleep

Being alone in this bed.

Through all the memories

And good times we've shared,

I cannot seem to shake the feeling,

That you never truly cared.

I'm alone, I'm dead

And I've been buried,

Buried alive in this

Concrete cemetery.

I need you now,

Like I never have before.

Striving to be with you,

Alas I'm still without,

It's too hard to move on.

Every day's a journey

Through turmoil and pain,

Things will never be how they were.

I don't even want them

To be the same.

Just give me the closure that I ask for,

Goodbye, see you on the next plane.

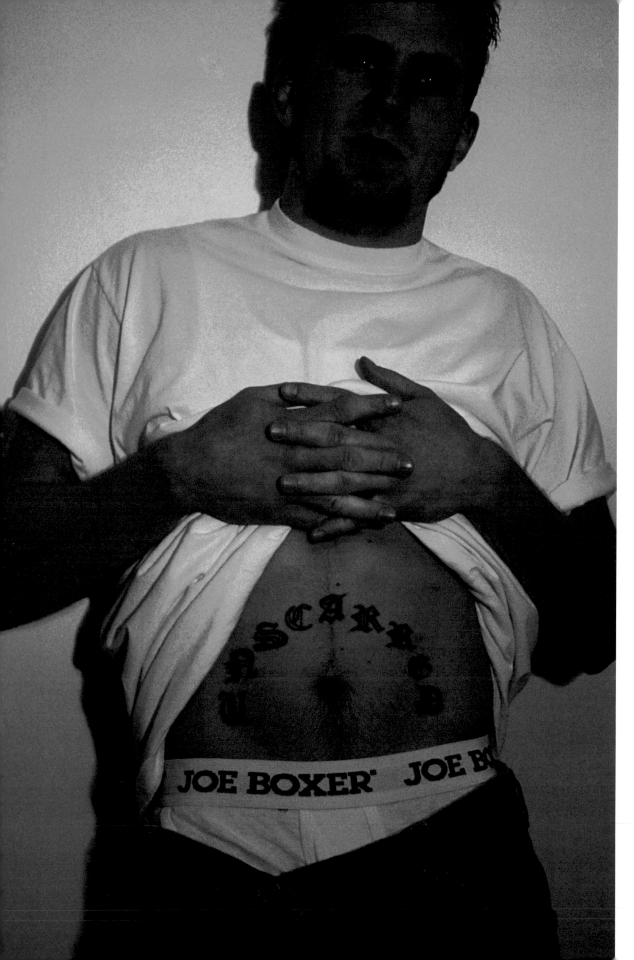

Myles Bolton

Born February 8, 1981
Sentenced for robbery,
armed robbery,
and assault, 2001
Regional Psychiatric Centre,
Saskatoon, Saskatchewan

Myles Bolton was born in Calgary and raised on Vancouver Island. He describes his early family life as filled with anger and violence, and says his first sentence to a correctional institution, for assaulting a schoolmate, occurred when he was twelve years old. Other arrests followed, for crimes including auto theft and robbery. At the age of fifteen Myles received his last sentence as a juvenile offender, for his part in the beating of a man which ended in the man's death. Released at the age of eighteen, Myles soon committed a series of assaults and robberies at ATM machines. He was arrested again just a few months after his release, and in 2001 was sentenced to eight years and eight months in prison.

Myles began serving his sentence in the maximum security Edmonton Institution. In 2003 he was sent to the Regional Psychiatric Centre (RPC) to complete an anger management program.

The RPC, comprised of a cluster of low buildings behind a vast parking area, stands directly across the highway from a large housing development. The Centre itself is set back at a distance from the main road so unobtrusively that on the day of our visit we first drove by without seeing it.

The RPC parking lot was nearly empty, and there were no other visitors as we entered the facility. We were led through a series of steel doors, past a plate glass-walled security room with banks of monitors, into the visitors' room, to set up our equipment. A corrections officer informed us there had been a disturbance in one of the units and a lockdown was currently in effect. But he assured us Myles was not involved in the disturbance and would still be allowed to take part in the interview.

When we met, Myles was soft-spoken and friendly; his manner relaxed and reflective. Before starting the interview, we photographed him both in the visitors' room and in the bitterly cold interior courtyard-garden adjacent to the room. Myles posed outside wearing only his indoor clothing, and we needed to take several trips inside to warm up between shots. He had brought a borrowed guitar with him, and after the photography and interview were over, he played some of his original compositions for us. His playing was understated and confident; his songs moody and melodic.

It was twilight when we left the RPC. Two members of the emergency response team who had responded to the earlier disturbance were leaving as we approached the reception area. Both were tall men wearing black fatigue uniforms. Both carried large, flat rectangular cases of the sort used to hold rifles. They joked with each other as they passed through the security checkpoint before us.

INTERVIEW: MYLES BOLTON

QUESTION: Just before we started recording you were talking about the seven circles of hell.

BOLTON: I just use that as an analogy, because my life ... it wasn't pleasant. Anger runs in the family, so to speak. I'm trying to stop it.

Q: Are you the only child?

B: Oh no; I have two brothers and a sister. I'm the eldest; that's why I took the most abuse. ... But I also antagonized a lot of it. I pushed the limits. You know, I'd sneak out or stay out late or I'd go out with friends and for one reason or another we'd get in trouble, whether it was breaking school windows or getting caught breaking into a place. I'd be caught and told not to hang out with those friends.

Q: Speaking of school ... how did you do in school?

B: Until grade nine it was kind of rough, because my home life was rough. I'd take a beating from my dad and go to school and beat some kids up just because. I got suspended a lot. But my grades were always good. So good in fact that I never did grade six. I went from grade five straight into grade seven. And then I never did grade eight; went straight into grade nine.

Q: Let's get to "Prison Ain't Much of a Place." Can we tell you something we did with your poem? We work in a school for really troubled kids with serious problems. But they're smart kids, and we gave one of the teachers your poem and asked him to read it. He read it, and then he used it in a class.

B: Cool!

Q: And the kids were completely knocked out by your writing.

B: That's cool! That brings tears to my eyes. I want nothing more than to help. ... You know what I mean? That means more to me than anything. I didn't think ... I didn't think anybody would appreciate it.

Q: In the poem you say one of the first people you see in prison looks like an All-Canadian College Boy, and then later you're disgusted because people outside have prejudices.

B: Have the same prejudices that I used to have. Look at me. Do I look like a convict? Probably not. I look like I should be in college. I could be in college on my lunch break doing something. ... I've got almost eight years under my belt, and it's kind of disgusting. 'Cause I know a lot of people on the street, they talk about cons, nasty, burly, scary-looking dudes. And they kind of just shun them all. "He's tainted. Keep him away from me." And I realized that I never really looked at myself that way, but up in the Max ... there's a lot of kids up there. Right now I think the average age is about twenty-four or twenty-five. But there's a lot of guys who are eighteen, nineteen, twenty years old ... and a lot of them are doing life. Because when you come in now, if you're doing a life sentence you have to do at least two years in Max. So everybody between Alberta and Manitoba who just picked up a life bit is going to Edmonton, and they're going to be there for at least two years.

The unit that I was living on, there's twenty-eight people, fourteen up, fourteen down. ... Upstairs it's usually old fellers, you know, old rounders, guys who have been in thirty, thirty-five, forty years. And on the other side it's guys my age who ... we're young, real young.

This one guy in particular ... he's a young guy, he's twenty, twenty-one, he's been in for a year and a half and he's got at least twenty-three and a half to go. I don't know what his trip was. I heard through the grapevine he killed his old lady. Hey, she must've really pissed you off to kill your old lady. He probably caught her cheating or something. I'm a bigger man, I turn around and walk away, say hey, have her, I'll trade her in for a new one. But I guess he couldn't do that. But this guy, he's so young, so innocent, he's so small. And that's when that first line hit me. You're supposed to be in high school or going to college. I'm like ... killed his old lady?

And then I turn around and I look at myself. Who the fuck am I to judge? You know? Look at what I've done to people in this world. I guess that's where that comes from. ... I'm young; I take it for granted that I've still got youth on my side but I also feel, on the inside anyway, I feel like an old man, because I've got a lot of time in. I see ... I call them kids, I'm only twenty-two myself but I see kids come in and I say, What are you doing here? You don't belong here. I know I don't belong here, but I can't do anything about it.

I like going in the sheriff's van because I'll always see guys that are doing provincial time, I see juvie kids and I'll lecture, I give them shit; I'll say, hey man, I ruined my life. I don't got fuck all. I don't get visits, no one to phone me. Everybody, all these people around here they got parents come and visit them, or they got family to send them money so they can buy tobacco or something. I don't. I got none of that. I'm sure that if I got out for a while I might be able to establish something; get my roots in the ground long enough so I could pick that up. You know I had an old lady and I don't know what happened to her.

Q: You said she stopped coming to see you.
B: Yeah. I used to get visits every two days. I'd call her on the off-days. Sometimes I wouldn't call her for a week because ... her work ... she had to do the night shift and I wouldn't call her. And one week she said, "Don't call me for a week ... I'll be on the night shift." I'm like okay, no problem, I love you. ... I called back when she asked me to, and she refused to accept my call.

Q: You said just before that if you're out for a while maybe you'll be able to establish some kind of kind of relationships like that, so that when you go back in you'll have somebody to visit you. Is that what you're planning? Is it the way you're thinking?
B: No. No. I didn't mean it to sound like that. I don't plan on coming back. I didn't plan on coming back this time. I really ... I honestly thought I got away with what I did, you know, because it was five months before I was arrested. And I ... it's not like I continued that behaviour. I wasn't using drugs, I'd been clean for years, except for weed but I don't consider that a drug. I don't drink; you know, I have the odd brandy or the odd scotch here and there. And I was working. I mean I was working sixteen, eighteen hours a day. ... I was juggling about four different jobs. One job I was driving a forklift in a warehouse. ... I'd do that on Monday, Tuesday, and Wednesday nights. On Thursday, Friday, and Saturday nights I usually worked in a restaurant.

Q: About your childhood ... you describe your childhood as being abusive, but you don't seem to dwell on it. You just state it like a fact.
B: It is a fact. I can't run from it. It's like ... I'm going to move on; because if I dwell on all that negative crap, it's just

dragging it around, and I've got a lot of stuff that I'm trying to deal with as it is. I mean as it is, my brain, it sends me into depression or it sends me into a state. I can't even really control it. I suffer from bipolar. A lot of people that suffer from bipolar use it as an excuse. "Oh, I get mad because this, or I freak out because this." Well you know what? There are lawyers, doctors, professors, judges. You know there are so many people out there that have bipolar disorder and function perfectly well. Why can't I? It still plagues me. It still bothers me. Until this morning, over this last week I've been really, really depressed. Really dismal, looking at the negative side of everything. But this morning I was really anxious because you guys were coming. This doesn't happen. This is a once-in-a-lifetime thing for me. So I kind of got my spirits up a bit. But I don't know, I'm still a little depressed, and it's really sad because I'm depressed about a girl that I loved who I haven't talked to in almost two years! And I'm still dragging it out, dragging it out, dragging it out in my head, right? And it's driving me insane. All I want is closure. ... I think I sent you a poem about closure.

Q: You say in "Prison Ain't Much of a Place" that you write letters, but you write fewer and fewer because you can't think of anything to say.
B: That's just exactly as it is. Say you're working in one place, in one job. It's a menial cubbyhole job like you see on TV or whatever. You come home, tell the wife ... she's like, "Hey, how's the day?" for your first few months. "Oh I did this, I did that, I did this." Then after, it just becomes so routine, so repetitious and so monotonous, you have nothing to talk about. Really, like if I was to have someone call me up and say "Hey! What'd you do yesterday?" "Uh I did the same thing I have been doing for the last

three years." It goes like that. But it's kind of fun to move around. Because when you get to a new institution you write everybody you know, "Hey, look, I'm here." And you get mail for a good three or four months, and then it dies off. Like I haven't gotten any mail for two weeks until today. ... For my first two months here, on the weekdays I got at least two pieces of mail every single day. And it starts to slowly trickle away. Now it's down. I get a letter every two or three weeks. That's just the way it is. There's nothing to talk about ... after you're settled in.

Q: In your poem you say you see men you respect. Who have you learned to respect?
B: Many other cons. Many other cons. Over the years you hear stories about guys, and I'm talking more or less about the old fellers, the guys who've got thirty-five years in. Like there's this one guy I know, I'm not going to use his name, but somebody was killed on the unit. He had absolutely nothing to do with it. And he went and he admitted to it. He took twenty-five years for that just to cover his friend's ass. He's now been in thirty-nine years. I don't really like the guy; but he has my utmost respect. There are stories like that all over the place.

Q: You say "Prison is a place where you see men that you respect then you start to wonder if you like them or not."
B: Well you can respect someone and not like them. Like that guy, I respect what he's done. I show him the most respect that I possess. I don't like him though. He's a bitter old grumpy dude. I seriously don't like even being near him. But I still respect him for the morals, the values and the ethics that he's held over the last four decades. I mean he's been in jail twice as long as I've

james

Me, Myself, and the Other Guy

wrigley

Me, Myself, and the Other Guy

I was very quiet about my history for a long time, although I am not specifically sure why that is; perhaps out of embarrassment or shame. My family always seemed more screwed up than most I heard about, and although I know I am not alone it cannot be said I share a norm with many. Until I was six my father lived with my mother, and from the outside I am sure it probably seemed fairly normal. I was the youngest of five and both my parents worked.

My oldest sibling, my brother Jack, was seventeen years older than I, and the next closest to me, my sister Sue-anne, was seven years my senior. Both parents worked for the school board, as did most of my extended family. When I was four we moved into a nice middle-class house in a new district that was growing. It was the 1970s and the job market was booming, which meant the city was changing fast, and all the urban problems were fairly new. My best friend lived next door and was the toughest kid for miles, which made me more cocky than I probably should have been. I was small and timid, and despite the many kids who lived on my block, kept myself fairly secluded.

I only barely grasped my parents' divorce and it really didn't affect who I was. I got to have two Christmases and two birthdays and gained two more sisters in the deal. Despite the beatings, the emotional abuse and riptides that tore through my family, I thought life to be normal. I of course knew little then and it wouldn't be until I was fourteen that I would question anything of what went on behind the cold walls of my two homes.

I got into trouble a lot around nine and ten, and soon gained a reputation within the neighbourhood. Parents didn't want their kids playing with me. Not all at once, mind you, but slowly people began to see me as a bad seed. I broke one friend's arm and was banned from playing at his house. Soon after, I was caught playing doctor at another kid's house and was banned from there. Stealing money, and getting kids to follow me into badly planned pranks and eventually shoplifting helped to cement the belief that people were better off not having me around. Years later, I wonder if it wasn't all simply a cry for help; a way to say I don't understand what is happening and being done to me. But really that seems more of a cop-out on responsibility than the truth.

When I was still a very young teenager I became involved in a relationship with an adult woman. I was invited a great many times to her apartment where she would feed me and play with me. I found solace in her, and love. As an adult I look back at the greatest love I ever had, and despite having sex with this person I never felt anything but protected by her. It is easy for me to say now that what I as a child

found myself in was wrong, but it never has, nor ever will take away from how much I was in love with her. I don't think of her in a romantic way anymore, and haven't for a very long time; yet it does not remove that her "abuse" was never violent or hurtful. It was never anything but nice.

I found myself in trouble early, as I have said, and I became a rebel without a cause, with few allies. After all, I was an independent, a mountain. I needed no one. That isolation was to assist me in separating myself from the rest of humanity, and although I never felt above them, I did feel removed. I tried drugs early and by fifteen found myself hundreds of miles from my "home" with a habit for experiment both with drugs and sex. I moved easily through the adult world for I was wanted and accepted by the many adults who needed just what I could offer. I used sex to bed older

women, to eat and have a roof over my head. When that would fail, I would turn to stealing what I needed or wanted, and soon I came to the attention of the youth criminal justice system.

By the time I was legally an adult I had a lengthy criminal record. I lived with a couple of women, always eight years my senior or older. However by that time I struggled for a level of normalcy. I started working more than stealing, and I had many jobs and many experiences as I travelled through this world. I was involved in everything from paramilitary groups to covens.

I became more refined, and more convinced that no one truly understood me except perhaps some of the women who shared my bed. My concepts of loyalty and honour were defined over these years and again I

found my reasoning and beliefs differing from mainstream society. I was forever an outcast, banished by my own fears and lack of understanding of why some things were as they were.

Then cocaine, or rather crack, entered onto centre stage of my life. Despite having a good job and even a relationship that was ending, but oddly stable, I dove deep into the next oblivion.

It was in the dark water there that I would commit the most horrendous crime I had ever chosen, as spite against the world. In the end I left a new chaos behind me. This one, however, did more than wound and worry,

it killed. For no reason other than the need of a vehicle and the puppet responses I willingly gave to another, I killed an old man. I did it as if not in my body and remember it as if I was more a spectator than a participant. Then I did everything within my power to say that it wasn't me. Some even believed me, but the police and the courts did not. As I stood in judgement, I was surrounded by faces I had seen using me and being used by me. These faces, however, had a voice and that voice committed me to life in prison.

I lived in a strange disbelief over the next few months, but gradually one thing occurred to me — and that was what I had done. Guilt flooded me, a guilt I could not even describe if I tried. Today, ten years later, I would like to believe I am the man I want to be, that the man ten years ago was nothing but a shadow of who I really am. But I can't detach myself from this one, not this time.

Every time I try to, I see the killer in the mirror.

In this brief telling of a thousand hurts and tears I hope I have done one thing — promote an understanding or insight into a fragile mind and heart. It should not make you feel pity or even empathy.

I am a creature who stalked the world in which you live.

Now I am a man who somehow wishes he could demand your forgiveness. But the truth is I should only get attention enough to stop it from happening to another; an example, if you will, of what not to do.

Love your children well, respect your neighbours as you would your family, and know that the bonds of family are more precious than winning an argument, or satisfying an urge. Don't agree with everyone — but tolerate that with which you cannot agree. And protect those who cannot defend themselves.

James Wrigley
Born October 21, 1969
Sentenced for second degree
murder and robbery, 1994
Drumheller Institution,
Drumheller, Alberta

James Wrigley was born and raised in Calgary, Alberta. He describes having had an outwardly middle-class upbringing but a chaotic family life scarred by sexual abuse, alcoholism, and divorce. Wrigley says he viewed himself as an outsider from a very early age. His conflicts with authorities began at an early age, too, and by the end of his teen years he had a record of convictions for a variety of crimes. Wrigley experimented with drugs, with right-wing racist groups, with fringe religious cults. Eventually he became addicted to crack cocaine. In the lowest depths of his addiction, he murdered an elderly Calgary man to steal his van for use in further crimes. Wrigley was sentenced to life in prison for this offense.

Drumheller Institution stands outside the town of Drumheller on the high prairies of Alberta. Our visit on a wintry late-November morning required a drive north from Calgary past frozen harvested fields that stretched golden and dazzling white to a limitless horizon. The open expanse of the region impresses visitors and residents alike: At dinner in a Drumheller restaurant, a young waitress told us a local joke about the prairies: "If your dog gets out, you can watch it run away for days."

Drumheller Institution sits in this vastness like an impenetrable fortress; a final stop. The grounds house both medium and minimum security facilities. Wrigley is confined in the medium security section. He, like many inmates, has attended classes at the Hilltop Education Centre, and that is where we were scheduled to see him. Located at the edge of the medium security facility, Hilltop Centre is an oasis: clean, well-lit, and orderly, bustling with focussed activity.

We met James Wrigley in a quiet classroom that had been reserved for our interview. Wrigley's manner was friendly and somewhat shy. As he talked about his childhood, his later life, and the crimes that brought him to Drumheller, he spoke softly, choosing his words with care. His tone was melancholy but without self-pity. We noted his fingertips were stained brown from heavy cigarette smoking.

Q: So you confessed to your mother?

W: Yes, and by saying it just to her alone, I think that was probably really the start.

Q: You've mentioned that your wife divorced you. At what point did that happen?

W: Just a little after the third year. At that time I was still waiting for the appeal of my sentence. I'm still doing life twenty-five. It's a sure twenty-five years. We just reached a, I'd love to say mutual, but I mean she needed to move on. ... She was hurt that I left her alone pregnant, and rightfully so.

Q: Was she pregnant when you were arrested?

W: She was. ... She was [left] raising my daughter on her own. I think she got so angry with me that she needed some kind of payment back. ... We were in the courts over custody.

Q: When you were in prison?

W: Yep. But I did it all through the lawyer. ... I was fighting so desperately to hold on to these last so very important things. ... They say you've got to hit bottom. That's not far from the truth.

Q: Do you feel like you've hit bottom?

W: Yes. I think that I was living a lifestyle and progressing so quickly that it could have easily ended up in my death and unfortunately ... tragically ... it took somebody else's [life] instead. ... Looking back at my lifestyle, if I had gotten away with it, there's nothing to say that it wouldn't eventually cost other people's lives, plus my own life. I mean certainly everything in [my] life was obviously out of control.

Q: You've been away from crack for nine years?

W: Yes.

Q: But it's available in prison.

W: Yeah, it is. I used it in the Vancouver Remand Centre; so it's more than ten years now since I've used any type of cocaine.

Q: Do you still feel the desire for it?

W: Oh yeah. If I see it on TV, if I see the substance. I've walked into a room where people are smoking it. You get that taste in the back of your throat. ... I haven't had them for a few years now but I used to have dream after dream after dream where I was constantly trying to get high off of cocaine and it wouldn't give me the buzz and I would get so angry with my dreams, they'd get me so frustrated and I'd need that buzz so bad. So I think that I will have a problem with cocaine all my life. The only good thing about it is that I fully know what the consequences are for me to say, "Ah, just once, won't hurt anybody." Because it would be just once in the beginning. ... When you're not sober it's easy, because it locks everything you care about. But on the other side, being sober, I know what that represents. ... So despite always wanting it, I'm never going to pay that price again. ... I think actually nicotine is probably a little more addictive drug. But ... you might get agitated or grumpy if you don't have your cigarette whereas with cocaine, you can kill.

Q: In your story you say that in your early days you never felt above humanity, but you did feel removed. How do you mean that?

W: The quip of the day is that you're unique just like everybody else. But back then ... I fit with very few people. Back when I was going to junior high school, the heads and the drug users were a very small group.

Q: You were a part of that?

W: Eventually. ... But I didn't really have too many close friends. Kind of a strange boy-meets-world. I guess between hiding things or feeling like I had to hide things, and just believing that my pain was different than everybody else's ... that [nobody] would understand.

Q: What is it you felt you had to hide?

W: Well, I mean my family was messed up, to say the least. Physical abuse, mental abuse, my mother was an alcoholic ... my father left the house. ... There was this terrible embarrassment that other people didn't have mothers like this, other people didn't have fathers like this. ... I was the egghead, I was the geek. ... There was this constant struggle for me just trying to be accepted by my peers. But it came to a point where even if they had started to accept me, I probably wouldn't have accepted them.

Q: You describe an early relationship with an older woman. Have you had any contact since you've been in prison?

W: No. I attempted a letter a couple of years ago but never received anything back. So I took that as a sign that she didn't want to remember, or didn't want to address me.

Q: How do you think that relationship influenced your choices in joining covens, racist groups, paramilitary groups?

W: I don't know. ... But I think that [relationship was] the only real safety net that I had. As I was getting older, it occurred to me that it was absolutely wrong. So I think I always so desperately sought another safety net, you know real love; and never could equate that sexual gratification and love were two distinctively different venues. So I guess I sought out groups that were on the fringes. They themselves were as desperate for people to come in, as I was looking for something to enter into.

Q: Did you see them as a cure or as part of the process?

W: Well I think that I saw them as normalcy, or an attempted normalcy, you know, a family, a friendship, a lifestyle. Of course for the most part ... every person in every group that I ever met were these terrible people that didn't have it together. For the most part, it was just from one dysfunctional thing to another and never acknowledging that there was anything wrong with it. ... It seemed perfectly normal to me.

Q: Have you been in such groups here?

W: No, I put that completely to the side.

Q: When you describe your process of remorse, you talk about "the killer in the mirror." How do you mean that?

W: I can't keep things at a distance anymore. I acknowledge that I have to keep them in the forefront of my life, and constantly under examination. That every time you think that maybe you're beyond that moment, you recognize that everything you are is because of that moment.

Q: The moment of the murder?

W: Yes. If I didn't kill somebody, if I just committed some robberies and got some jail time and went out again, I probably would have started the same pattern over and over again. ... It took this so black of a moment for me to wake up from the patterns, the beliefs that I had. The very person that I am, that I hate to acknowledge that I am, is the same person who is responsible for who I am now. So they're completely inseparable.

Q: You're saying that you constantly see yourself as a killer? You're constantly aware that you've killed?

W: Constantly aware is the best way of saying it. For a time, too, I was worried that because I crossed this line, could I even cross it again? I mean, it seemed like, you know, I have all these gradients in my life. I went to the fifteen-yard mark and then the next time I went to the twenty-five-yard mark and the next time the fifty and I get to this place where what worse could I have done? And the fear that would I be locked into a new pattern that would take me even beyond what I had already done.

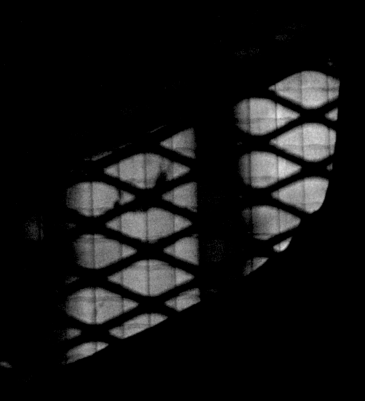

Q: Do you still have that fear?

W: No. Corny as it sounds ... I recognize that ... I'm responsible for the good or the bad I'm going to do tomorrow. It comes down to a simple choice. ... I think that I'm better about internalizing it. When I start to talk about it, it always sounds so shallow.... Even from being a child ... I was abused by the people that were supposed to love me, I was lied to by the people I was supposed to trust. I can remember ... I couldn't have been more than ten or eleven years old ... I remember thinking to myself that I wouldn't be that kind of father, that I would be there no matter what. I wanted to be a better man, a better person from what I saw around me.

Q: You mention concepts of loyalty and honour.

W: For me to have gone to a point where I committed ... I've been on the other end, so I can understand how it feels, like when he — the fear that he must have had, you know? To simplify it is to say that I inflicted on him some of the worst of what I learned, some of the worst that I'd ever felt, some of the worst that I'd ever seen. And in that moment, I became all the people that had ever hurt me, and I guess ... what bothers me so much is that I hold this ideal so proudly, so high. And inside of a moment, it didn't matter. ... That's something that's going to haunt me forever. ... I wanted to live life as the ideal pacifist, you know, that person that would look after other people that couldn't look after themselves. ... The one moment in my life that I probably should have been that person, was the one moment it utterly failed. And I can't separate myself from that [W pauses]. Near the beginning I had nightmares about [name deleted], who was my landlord.

Q: This is the first time you've mentioned the name of the man you killed.

W: He used to chase me in my dreams and all he kept asking me was, Why? Why did you do it? Why did you do it? I'm used to bad dreams but this was one of the many that scared the bejesus out of me for the longest time. And it's ... in a weird way, I mean, I don't [want to] make this sound like it's going to sound, but I'm looking forward, to a certain extent, that when I die, I'll finally be able to have the opportunity to allow him to confront me, then I'll be able to talk to him and tell him ... [W trails off]. He was an old man who couldn't defend himself even if he had tried. He didn't have a briefcase full of money, he didn't have — it was a dirty old van. ... It certainly wasn't worth his life, it certainly wasn't worth anyone's.

Q: You've said the same thing in your story.

W: I'd been writing that thing for probably five or six months and I'd write a paragraph and then delete it and then I'd rewrite another paragraph and slip it around a little bit, delete it again, then it was kind of a toss-up of ... it wasn't exactly what I wanted to say and at other times it was, "I don't know if I want to say that to anybody at all."

Q: Assuming you are always going to be seeing the same guy in the mirror, how do you want the rest of your life to go? What do you want to do?

W: Some people talk about the mansion on the hill and being independently wealthy. I'd be happy in a job that paid my bills and [if] I had a nice little home to go to, to watch my movies and watch my telly. I'm prepared, I guess now I want my niche within the framework of the community. I want to be able to volunteer in the community centre and have a decent job but nothing really beyond that. I don't need the gold bath fixtures anymore. I'd be happy just to have something that was mine. ▄

Maxine Fr
Lorri-Ann
Michelle Belc

Women of the Healing Lodge

The Okimaw Ohci Healing Lodge is a medium/minimum security prison opened in 1995 on the Nekaneet Reserve, near Maple Creek, Saskatchewan. Wide prairies crossed by highways and sectioned into fields and pastures surround the Lodge, but the facility itself lies in a birch woods among rolling hills. The Lodge houses about twenty women. Its mission statement says in part: "The Healing Lodge will promote a safe place for Aboriginal women offenders; an understanding of the transitory aspects of Aboriginal life; pride in surviving difficult backgrounds and personal experiences. The Healing Lodge will assist Aboriginal women as they begin their own individual healing process."

We visited the Lodge on a sunny morning in early winter. During the day we spent there with our three authors, and over the much longer time we spent working with our authors' written and spoken words, we came to believe the Okimaw Ohci Healing Lodge does as it promises.

DEAR COCAINE

By Lorri-Anne Cope

I am a twenty-five-year-old Aboriginal woman. I am currently doing a six-year sentence at the Okimaw Ohci Healing Lodge. When I came into the system, I was completely blind to my culture. Now that my mind and my spirit have been awoken to my culture, I feel like a different person. I wake up each morning thankful just to be alive. I don't take things for granted anymore. I am thankful for being an Aboriginal woman. I am also a proud mother and a strong sister and a loving daughter. I've learned about my self-worth, and how sacred we as Aboriginal women are. We have such strong power; we can give life.

Don't get me wrong: I've just found myself again; but this time I am more connected with my spiritual side. I had no idea how rich my people are until I got put in jail. My first smudge [the ritual burning of aromatic plants for purification — editors] was in Remand. My first sweat [a gathering where fire, smoke, and steam are used for spiritual cleansing and healing — editors] was in the pen.

I am thankful that I got picked up when I did — I am thankful now, that is. I can admit that at the beginning I didn't want change for myself. I guess I have found some hope for myself. I've done some things that I thought I could never forgive myself for, and I feel that one of the hardest things to do was to try, or even think about trying, to forgive myself. There, too, I found hope.

I have four beautiful children who are still waiting for me. I say "still waiting" because I asked my family to take them when I lost myself. I've been in for one year and I have one more to go until I get my day parole; but it has been three years since I've had my little ones in my care.

Prior to my incarceration I was on an extremely long binge. I got caught up in the "dope game." For all my fellow addicts, you know where I'm coming from; and for those who don't, I encourage you to educate yourselves about addictions. You never know when someone you love might get caught up.

The best thing for us addicts is to be honest with ourselves and our loved ones. If your loved one gets caught up and tells you, that's a cry for help. Be understanding and non-judgmental. All we want is someone to hear that cry for help, not get a door slammed in our face.

Anyway, I feel like I'm getting ahead of myself now. With this I would just like to encourage all my Aboriginal sisters and brothers to get involved with the Elders and the sweats. It's all part of our healing. For the people who are not Aboriginal and are curious about our ways, just ask and you too can get involved. In a way these ceremonies are like a church for us. I will leave you with this letter to my substance of choice. I will pray for all of us tonight, that we all find ourselves.

Dear Cocaine,

Hello, you know me pretty well and if you don't, I know you very well. At this point in my life, I don't miss you but at one point in my life I felt you were my only support. I'd like to say thank-you for helping me through my hard times. You helped me numb most of my hurt. You helped me forget most of my troubles but this was only temporary relief. We had quite the relationship and have done some crazy things together. You gave me power then that I would never need again.

Now see you as a weakness. Throughout your support I forgot my inner strengths and I also forgot how important I am to my loved ones. I became dependent on you. I wouldn't even let myself be dependent on a man but there you changed my standards. In the company of you I let almost all the things that were important to me slip away and none of that mattered to me as long as I had you. Then came the day that you were taken away from me and you were all I would think about. I can admit, yes, I did miss you. Then I realized where I was and why I was there. I began to think about reality and how wrong our relationship was. I began to think about what I let slip out of my reach and to be honest it was just about everything in my life. I know that if our paths were to cross again that I probably would have that thought about running away with you again. As of right now I am working on getting my inner strengths back and trying to understand how I let you get me the way you did. Once again I would like to thank you for being there for me when I felt that nobody else was. It was very unhealthy for me and I need to be healthy in mind, body, and soul for me and for my family. I know my children need me more than anything in this world. You've done what you could for me and now I have to do this on my own. So, with this I ask you to let me do this on my own and I ask you to let me find myself again.

Respectfully,
Lorri-Anne Cope

Although **Lorri-Anne Cope** was born to First Nations parents, she describes a childhood in which she learned little of her spiritual or cultural heritage. Lorri-Anne says by the time she was twelve years old she was cutting school, running away from home, and using drugs. She eventually became addicted to crack and drifted into prostitution. While deep in the underworld of cocaine use and crime, she took part in the armed robbery of a drug dealer. She was arrested and convicted for this, and eventually she asked to serve her sentence at the Okimaw Ohci Healing Lodge.

When we met with Lorri-Anne, she had been in the Lodge for about six months. Before meeting her we had been struck by the directness and openness of her writing, and over the course of our day together we came to see that her writing closely reflected her personality. Lorri-Anne spoke to us not with the fervor of a religious convert, but with the confidence of a woman who has awakened to her heritage, become aware of past mistakes, and gained an understanding of what she wishes her future path to be.

Lorri-Anne Cope
Born October 25, 1978
Sentenced for aggravated assault,
robbery with use of a firearm,
and possession of drugs for the
purpose of traffic, 2003
Okimaw Ohci Healing Lodge,
Maple Creek, Saskatchewan

INTERVIEW: LORRI-ANNE COPE

QUESTION: In your writing you say you were blind to your culture. How do you mean that?
COPE: I didn't even know anything about my culture. I was blind to it. ... I got so emotional with my first smudge I just started balling. It just felt so right for me, it just felt like that was what I was meant to be doing all my life. It felt like I was welcoming home my long lost sister or something. ... Right now I'm starting to learn more about the culture from the Elders here. I even have gone to the extent to get an Indian name. In our culture when you get an Indian name, that's like being baptized. ... Once you get on that path, if you get sidetracked, something bad will happen to you. You have to continue with this for the rest of your life in order for it to all work out in the end. I'm honoured to have an Indian name so I can do good with my life.

Q: What does your Indian name mean in English?
C: It means "Spring Sitting Woman." I've also got a colour; it's red.

Q: How did you come to write the poem "Dear Cocaine"?
C: It was something I had to write for the program. ... I went home and I wrote that poem up in about twenty minutes. Right before I went to bed, I just let it all out. When I woke up in the morning, I felt that I had to read it in class for some reason. And I couldn't help but cry. I wrote it about one of the teachings I received here about drugs, how we use them as medicine to cover up something. We try to self-medicate. We have to give thanks to these drugs for getting us through our hard times. So I wrote it all down. ... It was hard for me to read it because my voice was cracking. I wanted to just cry.

I took Aboriginal parenting here too and if I had known some of the things I learned here, I don't think I would have ended up the way I did. Now is my time. I'm young enough so I can turn my life around. I'm twenty-four years old, but I've been on the streets for half my life, since I was twelve. I know what's right and I know what's wrong now, and I'm only twenty-four. There's so much opportunity for me to change instead of carrying on with that cycle. Especially being a Native woman. We've been taught that we are sacred beings, that we give life. You can't mess around with that. If we don't have our spirituality, if we're not in touch with our spirit, then basically we have nothing, because if you forget about what's inside and who's in here, then you are numb to everything else that is going on around you. You don't care about what happens. And that's how I ended up. I ended up not worrying about my children. That's my main priority now, getting myself well so I can teach these little people how to be grown men. That's a big responsibility, to raise your child in a proper way. It's your chance to make up.

HEALING JOURNEY

By Michelle Bellecourt

I am a federally sentenced Aboriginal woman. Being sentenced to four years, eight months, I was sent to Saskatchewan Penitentiary Max unit for women. I had made the decision to change my life around, so I requested to come to the Healing Lodge.

Some may say that this is an easy place to do time, but for myself it was far from easy. Upon arrival here, I was a very angry woman and didn't know how to deal with my emotions. Being raised in a city, I had learned how to survive on the street. My lifestyle consisted of substance abuse and violence. I didn't know anything else and had accepted my fate.

My whole life has changed, as I was given the much-needed guidance to begin my healing journey. I not only opened my mind, but my heart too. As I received many teachings from the Elders I was able to participate in various ceremonies, from sweats to a four-day fast. I was even honoured in receiving my spiritual (Indian) name during one of the ceremonies I attended.

I am including a poem that I wrote while here. I feel it explains some of the things I have gone through. I know that my healing journey is a lifetime commitment and I accept that. I pray and smudge every day to the Creator to give me the strength to walk strong.

Healing Journey

Learning the honesty of my ways,
Will be hard on me some days.
Looking back in the past when I was a child
Realizing I was what you call a little wild.
Growing up a survivor was no easy task;
My emotions hidden behind a mask.
Knowing no other way of life;
Letting the hurt cut me like a knife.
Coping with it the only way I was able,
Is what you call pushing it under the table.
This way the pain being out of sight, out of mind,
I'd have time to look for a love I'd never find.
Thinking when I couldn't find it I was cursed.
Little did I know I had to love myself first.
Growing up is what I thought I had done.
But finding my inner child has been no fun.
From the beginning is where I must start,
Searching deep within my heart.
Beginning to care and nurture myself,
Instead of leaving it on the back shelf.
To bring forward my desires and needs,
Love is for what my inner child pleads.

I am working on all these new things,
And wait for each new day to see what it brings.
These days have brought a lot to me;
And my healing is the key.
With nothing to lose and everything to gain,
I have faced my hurts and inner pain.
As I have shed many tears,
I was able to confront my secret fears.
No longer caring what people think,
The wall around me started to shrink.
Knowing now I couldn't do this alone,
My attitude has taken a different tone.
I was able to open up and start sharing,
Because I found someone who is so caring.
I suppose that they were always there,
But being into myself I was unaware.
Regardless, I've taken the first steps of healing,
And with it comes so much feeling.
I am thankful to the Creator for each day,
And know he is with me in every way.

Michelle Belcourt describes a fragmented child-hood. For much of her young life she lived in a succession of foster homes, and she started running away from these homes as soon as she was able. Michelle experienced many aspects of homelessness in her teen years: living with friends, sleeping in parks and abandoned houses. Michelle was involved in gang life from an early age. She began drug and alcohol use early as well, and worked as a prostitute from the age of fifteen. In 2001 she was arrested for her part in the robbery of a convenience store. She asked to serve her sentence at the Okimaw Ohci Healing Lodge.

Michelle is unique among the authors in this book: With all the others, we first came to know them through their submitted writing, and only met them much later. We first came to know Michelle on the day of our visit to the Healing Lodge. As we were being given a tour of the Lodge, Michelle was working at a computer in the learning centre. We were introduced and talked briefly, and Michelle offered to show us a poem she had written. When we read "Healing Journey" we understood how important the Lodge was to Michelle, and we knew it was right for her to be part of this chapter.

Michelle Belcourt

Born April 7, 1971

Sentenced for forcible confinement, robbery, and possession of stolen property, 2001

Okimaw Ohci Healing Lodge, Maple Creek, Saskatchewan

INTERVIEW: MICHELLE BELCOURT

QUESTION: In your writing you talk about change being hard.
BELCOURT: It's hard because my whole life I've taken the easy way out, acting with violence and lashing out. Getting angry and not thinking, just doing. Not thinking about the consequences or the people I was going to hurt. I just wanted someone else to feel the pain that I was feeling. I wanted to project it somewhere else.

Q: Who would you lash out against?
B: Anybody. Anybody who looked at me the wrong way, anybody who said something wrong to me. I would find any excuse. They were just poor innocent people. I've dealt with that as part of my healing. I had to realize all the innocent people I hurt because I didn't want to feel pain, because I chose to project it somewhere else. ... So I did a ceremony for that, I prayed to their spirits. Even though they weren't physically dead, I prayed and asked their spirits to forgive me.

Q: Were you pretty much on the street when you were young?
B: Yeah, since I was about fourteen. I was raised in various foster homes but I always ran away. I was supposed to be living with my dad, my real father. I kind of laughed at him because the first month he tried to impose these rules on me but after a year on the street it wasn't happening [laughs].

Q: When you ran away where did you run to?
B: There was times where because I was supposed to be in school or my friends were supposed to be in school, I couldn't really run to my friends. I remember sleeping in abandoned buildings, sleeping in the park; hiding. They had those big tires; I hid there. I slept in abandoned cars. When my grandfather was alive he used to sell cars and one day he found me sleeping in one of his cars. He had a bunch of cars in the backyard because he had a big backyard. So after that, I would find one of the doors unlocked in one of the cars when I absolutely had nowhere else to sleep.

Q: Did you have to fend for yourself or did you run with a group of kids?
B: There was a group of kids but I pretty much had to fend for myself. And then I was introduced to prostitution. I was introduced to that really young, but I didn't start doing it myself until I was about fifteen.

Q: What were you sentenced for?

B: I pled guilty to robbery, unlawful confinement, and possession of stolen property. I was in on a robbery of a convenience store and the morning I woke up after it, I couldn't remember a lot of it. ... I took the store clerk hostage because I got mad at her. She froze from being scared but I thought she was just not listening to me, and that made me mad. ... I was swearing at her, "You think this is a joke." I just flew off the handle, and this poor woman … that's something else I've had to deal with. I wrote her a letter and said I was sorry. I don't know if she ever got it.

Q: Did you write the letter after you were sentenced?

B: Not right after, no. I think it was more when I made the commitment to change my life. It took me a long time sitting in the Remand, being locked up. ... I knew that something had to happen. And saying sorry to this woman was the first step for me. ... Now I remember most of that night and I remember her shaking with fear. It bothered me because I myself was trying to live what you would call a straight life. I was working in a convenience store. And I remember, like a week before I did this, I was closing up the store and a guy came in intoxicated. I thought he was going to rob me, and I remember how scared I got, and then I turned around and did this to someone else a week later. And not only did I rob her but I took her out of her safe environment.

Q: Did you have a weapon with you at the time?

B: I broke a bottle and used the broken bottle as a weapon. It took me a long time to remember that too. I still can't actually remember taking her out of the store. I can remember everything but that; I can't remember walking her out of the store.

Q: Do you find yourself remembering more and more?

B: Yes. Not just that time period but memories that I probably shut down my whole life are starting to come. I couldn't remember being younger than five years old. And now I can remember being three. And that's because I've given my whole being into my healing. That was something I was taught, as I heal more, I'll be able to remember more. And some of those memories are really hard.

Q: How are you doing that?

B: I did a lot of counselling. And a lot of it for me is my belief in prayer, in the smudge, in the sweat, in the ceremonies. For example, this morning I was hurting and the way I was taught was to let it go into the fire and ask the Creator to take it. And that's how I do things. I go into the sweat and I pray for the Creator to help me let it go. Otherwise it would eat me alive, and I don't want that anymore.

Q: Is your mom still alive?

B: Yep.

Q: Is she part of your life?

B: Nope, I don't think she ever was, except for the one year that she took us after we were put in an orphanage.

Q: What part does writing play for you?

B: Writing is my healing. For me, it's very therapeutic. I can start a poem and let out my emotions. And I can walk away from it and leave it unfinished, if that is what I need to do. I just write what comes [from my] heart. ... With my poem, I think that was my way of sharing.

Q: Did you share it with other people in class? Did the poem circulate?

B: Actually, yeah. I started off writing it. Then I put it in a newspaper ... and it was kind of funny because my roommate had a pen pal at Saskatoon Correctional and her pen pal sent her a copy of their newsletter. It turns out they had taken my poem out of the newspaper and put it in the Saskatoon Correctional newsletter. So it was just making its rounds.

Q: How did you feel, knowing that the poem was making the rounds?

B: At first I was really shy about it because I'm a known gang member in Edmonton. You know being a gang member I had to be violent, and I had to portray myself being hardcore. I wasn't allowed to have feelings. I finally took the risk and shared it with one of the [gang members], and the response ... he said I was his inspiration. That if I could change, then why couldn't he?

B: Yes. He must have shared it with another one, because I got another letter and they started encouraging me to continue on my journey and not go back to the lifestyle. Then all of a sudden they admitted that they prayed. It's like, "Don't tell anybody, but I pray at night." Some people are shocked because I actually showed them that I had a heart. I can open that door, even if it's just a crack.

Q: Did you have a lot of people frightened of you?

B: I was the queen of intimidation. And that's something else I have to let go of — the guilt. I remember this one time, I was in a 7-Eleven store and I was drunk. I was with another gang member and this guy just wanted to be our friend, because he knew who we were. He didn't know exactly, he just knew which gang we were. And he was just trying to be our friend, and he said something that made me mad, and I ended up stabbing him five times. Just because he made me mad. I fed his spirit too.

Q: What happened to him?

B: He lived, that's all I know. I remember I thought at the time he was so solid because he didn't tell the police. So my first reaction, my first thought about it was, "Well, at least he's solid and didn't rat me out." Never mind how good is he doing, is he okay. You know I think about things like that now. ... All the people that did try to reach out to me, I just shit on them. I'm really happy I'm not that person anymore.

Q: Have you had to develop a different set of skills to be this new person?

B: They were probably already there. It's just letting them come out and letting them be positive. Changing that negative to a positive. ... I think of the consequences now. Before, I could care less. When I'd be in Remand and they'd send me to the hole or whatever, I'd stand in the middle of the room and say, "Bring it on" — not caring if I was going to get beat up by the guards or whatever. Now I think about it. Because it's not going to hurt anybody but me. PV

THE HORSE PROGRAM

By Maxine Friesen

I'm a repeat federal offender serving a second sentence, for drug trafficking. I would like to disclose my personal experience attending the Horse Program offered to inmates at the Okimaw Ohci Healing Lodge, near Maple Creek, Saskatchewan, on the Nekaneet Reserve.

The Horse Program started September first, and lasted thirty days. The first morning began with a sharing circle. The Elders John and Margaret Oakes opened our circle with a smudge and a prayer. We each spoke, letting the group know what we were expecting and how we were feeling about being in the program. After the morning circle, we talked about the sweat lodge ceremony that was to take place that afternoon. One of the program facilitators, along with the Elder, gave us a teaching on the sweat lodge and why ribbons, tobacco and prints were offered in the sweat lodge. We learned they were for the Horse Spirit to protect us and to help us show respect for the horses.

To prepare for the horses' arrival, we cleaned out the barn, the stalls, and the corral, which had large branches strewn throughout. We took out thistles and burrs from the corral because they could be harmful to horses. Everyone was excited when the horses arrived the next day.

I had a lot going on in my life at that time. My mother had been in the hospital on and off for several months. She'd had open-heart surgery in August. I was eligible for unsupervised temporary absences and was able to go see my mother before and after her surgery. Even though she started recovering, by September she had taken a turn for the worse and had another surgery. I had been waiting for news of her condition and always spoke about her to the group.

In the second week, a member of the local community, Bill Keaton, presented the women of the Healing Lodge with a horse. We planned a ceremony for two days later, when Mr. Keaton was to bring the horse to the Healing Lodge. The Elder John Oakes suggested to the women that they learn the Horse Spirit Honour Song, to sing when receiving the horse. Elder John Oakes sang the song for me to learn and teach the other women. I was allowed to tape record him. Harry Frances sang a Thank-You Song, which I recorded at the same time. But no one else could get the words (sounds). After five hours of practice, everyone else gave up trying and went home.

Maxine Friesen with Nekaneet Elders Margaret and John Oakes

The next day Rick Ratte from Aboriginal Peoples Television Network was present. I was asked if I would do an interview on videotape. I was honoured to be asked. I did the interview and found it extremely intense, touching feelings I had long put to rest. The new horse was brought in that same afternoon. I had to sing the Horse Spirit Honour Song at this ceremony. I was also asked to wear a microphone, to be videotaped by APTN.

In the third week, I was called aside by staff at the Healing Lodge and with the Elder present I was told that my mother was gone. She had grown slowly worse after her second surgery. My mother passed away on the evening of September 16. My plans had been to leave the Healing Lodge and stay with my mother to assist in her recovery as my statutory release was coming up in November.

I was very close to my mother, although we had to repair a very dysfunctional relationship due to alcohol and drug abuse. My father had passed away twelve years before this and the bond between me and my mother had grown stronger in this time period. My mother was a role model for me: She had overcome her addiction to alcohol. She had become a strong and dependable woman for her ten children, numerous grandchildren and great-grandchildren. I was devastated, hurt, and lonely for my family.

I listened to the teachings I was given by all the Elders, which helped me deal with the overwhelming grief I was experiencing. The afternoon I was scheduled to leave to visit with my family, the instructor told me to go ahead and take a horse for a ride. The horse I had bonded with was Medicine Flash. She had only been around for several weeks, although she was given to the Healing Lodge the year before. I'll never forget that ride. I felt as if Medicine Flash understood every sad feeling I was experiencing. My tears began to fall as I rode one last time around the corral.

I left the Healing Lodge that day to attend my mother's funeral in northern Alberta. Those were the longest seventy- two hours I had ever experienced in my life. Also one of the hardest times emotionally and spiritually. I took one of the drums from here at the Healing Lodge, and sage to smudge with, knowing full well these two items would be my only hope of some sanity on this trip. I thought many times of the horses and my group back at the Healing Lodge.

The last week of the Horse Program, the video interview I had done for APTN was played in group on a Tuesday morning. Our lodge mother (warden) had taped it and brought it in for us to watch. It was really strange to see myself at what I felt was a high level of spirituality. I kept telling myself, "Believe it, Maxine, that is who you are now."

Acceptance of one's self is a huge step and can be an awakening for the soul. I choose to believe that my commitment to change and spiritual awakening, which came from the sweat lodge ceremonies and the sundance ceremony, took me to a place of peace and serenity while in my darkest moments of grief. I will be eternally grateful for the Horse Program.

Maxine Friesen

Born July 7, 1961
Sentenced for possession of drugs for the purpose of traffic, document forgery, theft, and failure to appear in court, 2002
Okimaw Ohci Healing Lodge, Maple Creek, Saskatchewan

Maxine Friesen describes growing up in a large family devastated by alcoholism. She says she took on much of the responsibility for the care of her siblings at an early age, but left home for good while still a young teenager. Although Maxine soon began a family of her own, she speaks of the last twenty-five years as a constant struggle between conflicting urges: her desire to be a good mother clashing with her needs as a drug addict and dealer. She served a sentence for armed robbery before her current sentence for drug trafficking and other crimes.

We spoke with Maxine in the mid-morning of our visit to the Healing Lodge, in a playroom used by children during family visits. The playroom was sunny and cheerful, filled with brightly coloured school equipment. There were full-size chairs available, but we all chose to sit in children's chairs at an activities table. Maxine spoke earnestly, as if vividly recalling each of the times, places, and people she described. In her words and manner she gave the impression of having reached a turning point in her life, of having attained a high degree of understanding and peace. On the day of our interview, Maxine was one week from being released.

INTERVIEW: MAXINE FRIESEN

QUESTION: You left home when you were very young. Tell us how it happened.

FRIESEN: My older sister [had already] left, and I was kind of stuck holding everything together. When I was thirteen my whole family moved into one of the slummiest housing places in Grand Prairie. My mom's drinking just got worse and worse. I remember her waking me up the actual night I left home. She brought a bunch of people home who were drinking. My little sister, she was only three years old, woke up and was crying and she came running out of the bedroom. I was up cooking for all of these people. She came running up to me and was hanging onto the sleeve of my nightgown and she was saying, "Mommy, Mommy." She was calling me Mommy, and my mother just flipped right out. I got thrown out of the house. She was saying, "You're not taking my family away from me!" She was just out of control.

Q: What grade were you in when you left school?

F: Grade ten. I loved school; it was like an escape. I remember loving English the most because we had such a good English teacher... just the way she put words together. She used to read us stories in class, and I would just get lost in these stories. They were so beautiful, about wonderful things happening, and love and kindness. All the things that I was missing in my life.

Q: When did you discover writing?

F: I always liked writing. ... I guess when I was really hurt, I started going through some painful things, and I started putting it all down on paper. I remember I had a whole scrapbook filled completely with poems and little stories and thoughts about how I was feeling. One of my sisters got hold of it and read it, and she thought I was ready to commit suicide [laughs]. Those were just my feelings. How could I get that out of me if I didn't express it in some way?

Q: When you left home, where did you go?

F: Actually, the night I left home a carload full of hippies picked me up. It was the early '70s. And they took me out to this farm about fifty miles outside of Grand Prairie. They used to call it Hippie Hill. Not too many people knew about it. I stayed there for the first seven or eight months and baby-sat for these people. They were probably doing some things that were illegal, and smoking some things they shouldn't have, but I was safe. It was a safe place to live.

Q: And after those eight months?

F: I met a guy. I was fourteen, and we stayed together until I was eighteen.

Q: You eventually got out of Grand Prairie?

F: I spent two years in America. I went down with the father of my two children. We were going to get things together. He ended up pulling an armed robbery and doing some time down there. My kids actually got taken away from me. This man was very abusive, he was very controlling, and I found myself lost without him. I finally made it back to Canada, and my sister had taken my kids for me.

Q: What happened when you returned to Canada?

F: I turned into a super mom. I had met another man in 1990, and we had another child in 1991. We met at a sawmill in High Prairie. But that relationship fell apart after my dad died. My dad died at home of lung cancer. Almost a year to the day before my dad passed away he'd phoned me. It was late but he was all excited, saying "Maxine, Maxine, guess what I saw?" He used to phone me about every night. He said, "I was driving down the road, and right in the middle of the road there was an owl. It was four feet high and it just stood there, and I had to slam on the brakes. I skidded towards it and it flew right up over the truck." In the Aboriginal culture, the owl is a messenger of death — depending on how it presents itself. I remember going silent on the phone. Within a year, his mother, my cousin, and my father all passed away.

Q: What drugs were you involved with?

P: Heroin. But cocaine as well. The charge I'm in for is trafficking crack cocaine. I mean I was using it, but my own supply was heroin.

Q: How did you come to the Healing Lodge?

F: I felt really bad before I even got to the point where I was willing to come here. My first sentence was for armed robbery. I robbed a drugstore to get synthetic heroin. The person that I've become since 1997... it has been seven years ... I've changed so much. But it wasn't overnight. Packing a sawed-off gun and pulling armed robberies to stay high seven years ago ... that took a lot of changing. On top of everything, I think because of all the hurt and the sexual abuse, I had a sexual relationship with another woman. That was who I was with when I did the armed robbery. We went to the pen together. We fought for gay rights. We got the first private family visit that a gay family ever got. When I got out, she was so far behind me emotionally. ... We're still friends, but that relationship ended in 1999, right after I got out. I was doing really well. I had worked really hard at work release. I was in a training program and then I got hired full-time through Ability Training in Alberta. ... I got a back injury. I honestly didn't think I'd go back to using, but I ended up in the hospital and got on painkillers. It just started my addiction all over again. ... After having a job in the federal office, and then to find out a year and a half later that it was all for naught once my addiction was started again.

Q: The Elders here, Johnny and Margaret, asked to adopt you. How were they motivated to do that?

F: I've gone to every sweat since I've been here. I've been really sincere in asking questions and wanting to change. They've watched me develop and change into the person sitting here today. When I walked in here a year ago, my hair was red and it was all chopped off. I was just mean and miserable. I knew that I wanted something different. I wasn't prepared to have my sentence end at Edmonton [Institution for Women] and go back out with a kind of mentality that wasn't really positive for myself or anyone else around me. I wanted something, and I think I found it here.

Q: How do you think the Lodge helped you?

F: The Elders, the programs, the serenity. ... My place looks out to those trees right along there. There are days and days and weeks and weeks that I'll just sit out and look at those trees. Moose come to my doorstep. Having lots of time to understand and comprehend. As well as in my school ... working on my understanding, allowing myself to believe that I could do something if I really applied myself.

Q: So here there's serenity and strength. But in a week you are going back out. How do you think you are going to do?

F: I think I'm going to do really well because it's not about people-pleasing anymore. It's not about what I can do for other people anymore. ... My whole life, that's what I did real well: take care of everything, take care of everybody else. I wasn't taking care of me. If I love myself, and give myself and my life that much attention, I truly believe it's going to take a whole new turn.

Q: Let's talk about the horse program that you wrote about. What was the most intense part of it for you?

F: The sweats ... being in the circles and praying ... and spending time with the horses. ... Right around the time my mom passed away, [one of the teachers] was going to show us how to get a horse if it was going around really fast and you couldn't catch it; how to soothe it and get it to calm down. He had this one horse that had never been around people and was kind of fidgety, and he said, "Someone come in and I'll show you [how] to catch it." He was so disappointed because I walked right up to the horse and put my arms around him and kissed him. And the teacher was looking at me like, "Why did you have to do that? I can't use this horse now" [laughs]. But it was like the horse was scared. And I knew he was scared. And I didn't want him to be scared. ◪

MARIO

AUGER

UN ENFANT DE 7 ANS
A CHILD OF 7 YEARS

UN ENFANT DE 7 ANS

Depuis quelques semaines, je suis retourné à l'école. J'ai recommencé au présecondaire ; après seulement quelques jours je me suis rendu compte que je pouvais écrire moi aussi en limitant mes fautes. Alors, j'ai multiplié mes efforts. J'avais beaucoup de difficultés à écrire et à lire dès le début du primaire. J'ai toujours cru que j'étais incapable de réussir à l'école. Voilà, aujourd'hui, je peux réussir.

Prenez quelques minutes avec moi si vous voulez bien. Je vais vous conduire sur le chemin de mon enfance. À l'âge de 7 ans, mes parents ont divorcé. Alors avec ma mère et mon frère, nous avons déménagé dans un quartier pauvre d'une ville. Dès le début des classes, j'ai eu de la difficulté. Ma mère est la beauté même, elle me donnait tout l'amour qu'une mère peut donner à son fils. Mais la vie a été très dure pour elle. Elle s'est retrouvée seule avec deux jeunes enfants. Alors, je me suis retrouvé seul avec mes échecs. J'ai grandi avec l'idée que je ne pouvais pas réussir mes dictées. Personne ne m'a pris la main pour me conduire vers ces classes où j'aurais pu réussir mes dictées.

Je me suis fait des nouveaux amis dans ce quartier. Le soir, nous allions nous promener dans les rues. Alors mes dictées et mes examens, j'allais les passer dans les rues, là j'ai eu des bonnes notes. Il s'est formé une petite gang, moi j'étais le plus jeune et le moins dur. Ils ne voulaient pas de moi, avec le temps j'ai fait mes preuves, je me suis endurci.

À l'âge de 7 ans, je marchais déjà sur ce chemin qui m'a conduit entre ces barreaux. Dans mon cœur d'enfant, je voulais seulement avoir mon père près de moi, avoir un support pour mes études. Participer à des loisirs avec des jeunes de mon âge. J'ai appris à vivre au lieu dans un milieu où vivent le mensonge, la haine, le crime. Mes nouveaux amis vivaient dans des familles où la pauvreté était là à tous les jours. Leurs idoles étaient des vieux criminels du quartier, qui sont devenus les miens avec le temps.

Je connaissais seulement des échecs. Je cherchais, je me cherchais dans ce milieu. Je ne pouvais pas comprendre les conséquences de ces échecs sur mon avenir. Dans mon cœur d'enfant, la première graine de tritesse était semée depuis le premier échec avec mes dictées. À l'âge de 11 ans, je faisais déjà partie d'un autre monde où vit le crime, avec les premiers vols dans les dépanneurs, les premières cigarettes. Moi, ce jeune garcon, je voulais seulement jouer et découvrir la vie qui s'ouvrait devant moi. J'avais besoin de me valoriser de me trouver une identité, un point pour me rattacher. Laissé seul à moi-même dans la rue, j'ai appris à vivre avec ses règles. Jour après jour, je me suis fait une réalité de la vie. Moi aussi, j'ai eu mes premiers rêves, mais ils ont fait place à la réalité de mon chemin.

A CHILD OF 7 YEARS

A few weeks ago, I went back to school. I restarted at the pre-secondary level. After a few days, I realized that I, too, could write, by being careful. So, I doubled my efforts. Ever since starting elementary school, it was very difficult for me to read and write. I always thought that I could never succeed in school. And yet, today I can succeed!

Spend a few minutes with me. I will lead you on the path of my childhood. My parents divorced when I was seven. With my mother and brother, we moved to a poor neighbourhood. From the very beginning, I had difficulty in school. My mother was tired of life. I was all alone with my failures. I grew up thinking that I could not succeed in school. No one took my hand to lead me towards classes that could have helped me pass my examinations. I made new friends in this neighbourhood. In the evenings, we would go hang out in the streets, so I took my exams in the streets at night and I got good grades. We started a small gang. They did not want me because I was the youngest and the least tough. With time, I proved myself and hardened. At the age of seven, I was already walking on the path that led me behind these bars.

In my young heart, I only wanted to have my father close to me, have some support for my schooling, participate in activities with kids my own age. I learned to live in this world of lies, hatred, and crime. My new friends all lived in families where poverty was an everyday reality. Their idols were old criminals from the neighbourhood; with time, they became my idols too.

In school I only knew failure. I was looking; I was trying to find myself in this environment. I could not understand the consequences of my failures on my future. In my young heart the first seed of sadness had been sown with the first failure of school tests. At the age of eleven, I was already part of this other world of crime: first thefts in convenience stores, first cigarettes. I was a young boy who only wanted to play, discover life that was opening up in front of me. I needed to feel valued, to find an identity, an "anchoring point." Left to my own in the street, I learned to live by its rules. Day after day, I learned the reality of life. I, too, had my first dreams, but they made way for the reality of my road.

J'ai fini par réussir mon primaire avec quelques années en retard. Là au secondaire, libre ! On peut faire ce qu'on veut. Au lieu de travailler dans mes livres ou d'aller en classe, j'allais fumer du pot. Notre gang prenait forme, avec des vols plus fréquents, j'avais laissé tomber les vols de dépanneurs pour les vols de maisons. Mon ambition était de devenir le plus dur de la gang, le meilleur voleur de mon quartier. C'est sur ce chemin là que moi, ce jeune garcon, ai trouvé un point d'attache qui est devenu moi.

Là, rendu 22 ans plus tard, je suis assis sur une chaise de retour en classe. Depuis quelques mois, je suis retourné à l'école. J'ai recommencé au niveau du primaire. Les premières journées étaient très difficiles pour moi. Avec l'aide de mon professeur et de la persévérance de ma part, j'ai découvert le plaisir de jouer avec les lettres. Après seulement deux mois en classe, il y a eu des progrès surprenants. De constater que je pouvais réussir en classe m'a rendu heureux et en même temps triste.

HEUREUX, de pouvoir écrire à mes enfants, mon épouse et mes amis. Le désir d'aller voir plus loin ce que je vais découvrir, surtout de voir que moi, le petit garçon 22 ans plus tard, je pouvais réussir mes dictées.

I finally completed elementary school, a few years late. Now in secondary school, I was free! I could do whatever I wanted. Instead of studying my books or going to school, I would go and smoke pot. Our gang was taking shape, with more and more thefts. I moved from convenience stores to house burglaries. My ambition was to become the best and toughest burglar in my neighbourhood. It is on that road that the little boy I was found his anchoring point.

Here, twenty-two years later, I am sitting at a school desk. I have been here for a few months. I restarted at the elementary level. The first days were very difficult. With the help of my teacher and perseverance on my part, I discovered the pleasure of playing with letters. In just a couple of months I made surprising progress. Realizing that I could succeed in school made me both happy and sad.

Happy to be able to write to my children, my wife, and my friends. Wanting to go further and discover more. Mostly to see that, twenty-two years later, the little boy that I was can pass his exams.

Sad: I am sitting here, looking out the window. I see the bars that separate me from those I love. Among the several questions that are looking for answers, one wants an answer at any price: "If the young boy had passed his exams at the age of seven, would his anchoring point have been different all along his path?"

TRISTE, là je suis assis, je regarde la fenêtre de ma classe, je vois les barreaux qui me séparent de ceux que j'aime. Il y a plusieurs questions qui cherchent des réponses, mais il y n'a une qui veut avoir une réponse à tout prix. « Ce jeune garçon à l'âge de 7 ans, s'il avait réussi ses dictées, est-ce que son point d'attache aurait été différent tout au long de son chemin ? »

Je pourrais vous écrire bien d'autres événements que j'ai vécus tout au long de ces 34 ans. Il y a des très beaux moments, j'ai une épouse qui m'aime, deux jolis enfants. J'ai fait des voyages dans quelques pays. J'ai des moments plus noirs que j'ai vécus. J'ai passé plusieurs années au centre d'accueil et en prison tout au long de ces 34 ans. Là, il me reste quelques années à faire avant de retrouver ma liberté.

La question est toujours là, pas de réponse. C'est pas grave, je peux poursuivre mon chemin quant même, je suis un gars de la rue, je suis un dur. Aujourd'hui, je vais vous dire un secret caché loin des regards – ça fait mal d'être en prison loin de ceux que j'aime et de penser aux chagrins que je peux leur avoir fait.

À vous ce que je veux vous dire : Demain, quand vous serez sur la route pour aller à votre travail, regardez ce jeune enfant de 7 ans qui attend l'autobus pour aller à son école. Demandez-vous ce que ce jeune peut bien vivre, quel chemin il va suivre tout au long de sa vie ? Ce jeune, ces jeunes enfants vont prendre un chemin ou l'autre sans comprendre l'importance que cela aura tout au long de leur vie.

Il reste ma question, je vous laisse le plaisir d'y répondre pour moi : SI J'AVAIS RÉUSSI MES DICTÉES, QUEL AURAIT ÉTÉ MON POINT D'ATTACHE ?

I could write about many other events that I have lived through. There have been some very beautiful moments: I have a wife who loves me and two beautiful children; I have travelled to a few countries. And I have also lived through some darker moments. I have spent several years in group homes and prison; I have to spend a few more years here before I regain my freedom.

The question still remains, with no answer. It doesn't matter, I can continue on my way, I am streetwise, I am tough. Today I am going to tell you a well-hidden secret: It hurts to be in jail, far from those I love, and to think about the sorrows that I caused them.

I want to tell you this: Tomorrow when you are on your way to work, look at the young boy of seven who is waiting for the school bus. Ask yourself what this boy is going through; what path will he follow through life? This boy, these boys will take one path or another without understanding the importance it will have on their lives.

My question remains; I let you answer it for me. If I had passed my examinations, what would have been my path, my anchoring point? A child, who became an inmate: Mario Auger.

Le mensonge

Un garçon arrive en courant chez lui ;

« Maman ! Maman ! Un petit oiseau est tombé de son nid. »

Sa mère se retourne, le regarde quelques instants puis reprend ses occupations. Le garçon la regarde et ne comprend pas son attitude. Il reprend sa course vers son père qui bricole.

« Papa ! Papa ! J'ai vu un petit oiseau tomber de son nid ; viens vite, le chat va le manger. »

« Je suis occupé »,

Répond son père.

Il voit son grand-père lire son journal.

« Peux-tu venir avec moi grand-père ? Il y a un oiseau seul qui a perdu sa maison. »

« Non, Je lis mon journal »,

Lui répond son grand-père.

Le garçon se retourne et prend la direction de sa chambre, il gravit l'escalier pas à pas, son cœur se remplit de chagrin. Les larmes coulent sur ses joues à l'idée de laisser le petit oiseau seul loin de sa maison. Sa petite soeur le voit pleurer, elle s'approche de lui et lui demande :

« Pourquoi pleures-tu ? »

« Laisse-moi seul, tu es trop petite pour comprendre. »

« Mon frère, même si je suis petite, je peux comprendre bien des choses. Pourquoi pleures-tu ? »

Les larmes coulent sur le visage du petit garçon et il lui répond :

The Lie

A boy arrives home running: "Mommy! Mommy! A little bird fell from his nest."

His mother turns around, looks at him for a while and goes back to what she was doing. The little boy doesn't understand her attitude. He runs towards his dad, who is fixing something. "Daddy! Daddy! I saw a little bird fall off his nest. Come quick; the cat is going to eat him."

"I am very busy," his dad answers.

He sees his grandfather reading the paper. "Can you come with me, Grandpa? I saw a bird alone, lost from his home." "No, I am reading the paper," his grandfather answers. The little boy turns around, climbs up the stairs towards his room, step by step, his heart heavy with sorrow. Tears are running down his cheeks as he thinks about the lonely little bird away from his home. His little sister sees him crying, comes near him and asks, "Why are you crying?"

"Leave me alone, you are too young to understand."

"Brother, even if I am young, I can understand things. Why are you crying?"

« Il y a un petit oiseau qui va mourir et personne ne veut venir avec moi pour l'aider à retourner dans sa maison, et toi tu es trop petite ».

Sa soeur prend sa main, l'entraîne à l'extérieur en lui disant :

« Viens ! Viens ! À nous deux, on va réussir à le sauver ».

En route vers le petit oiseau, la petite soeur pose des questions à son grand frère :

« Maman, papa et grand-père n'ont pas voulu venir avec toi sauver le petit oiseau, pourquoi ? »

« Arrête de poser des questions et dépêche toi. »

Peu à peu la petite soeur commence à prendre du retard sur son frère. Elle s'arrête brusquement et lui dit :

« Arrête ! Je veux te parler, mon frère, viens près de moi ».

Il se tourne vers sa soeur et voit son regard le suppliant de venir lui parler et lui répond :

« Ok ! Mais fais vite ».

« J'ai entendu parler maman et papa hier ; ils parlaient de toi, mon frère. Ils ne savent plus quoi penser de toi, ils ont remarqué depuis quelque temps que tu contes des mensonges. »

Le garçon se retourne sans dire un mot et reprend sa marche dans le sentier en direction du petit oiseau.

Ils arrivent près de l'arbre où l'oiseau est tombé, le cherchent, mais en vain ;

« Il est arrivé malheur au petit oiseau »,

S'inquiète le frère.

« Petit garçon ! Petit garçon ! Regarde vers le ciel, dans la branche de l'arbre. Je suis la maman du petit oiseau que tu as

Tears are running down the little boy's face as he answers: "There is a little bird that is going to die and no one wants to come with me to help him return to his home, and you are too young."

His sister takes his hand, pulls him outside while saying, "Come! Come! Between the two of us, we can do it."

On their way, the little sister asks questions to her big brother: "Why did Mommy, Daddy, and Grandpa not want to help you save him?"

"Stop asking questions and hurry."

Little by little, the little girl starts to fall behind her brother. She suddenly stops and says, "Stop! I want to talk to you. Come near me, brother."

He turns towards her and sees her look begging him to come and talk. "OK! But hurry."

"I heard Mommy and Daddy talking about you yesterday. They don't know what to think of you. They have noticed that you have been telling lies for some time." The boy turns around without a word and starts walking on the path towards the bird. They arrive near the tree where the bird had fallen and look for him in vain. "Something terrible happened to the little bird," worries the little boy.

"Little boy! Little boy! Look towards the sky, in the tree branch. I am the mother of the little bird that you wanted to save; I want to thank you for the concern you had for my baby. He told me that you would come back to help with an adult. Where is the adult? I want to thank him too."

voulu sauver. Je veux te remercier pour l'attention que tu as eue pour mon petit bébé. Il m'a dit que tu reviendrais l'aider avec une grande personne. Où est cette grande personne que je la remercie aussi ? »

La petite fille répond à la maman oiseau :

« Moi je suis là et je suis grande, j'ai 4 ans ».

Puis le petit frère reprend la conversation :

« Personne ne m'a cru, ils ont tout pensé que je leur racontais un mensonge ».

« Pourquoi crois-tu qu'il ont pensé cela ? »,

Demanda la maman oiseau.

Le petit garçon hésita, baissa la tête et son visage rougit de honte :

« Maman oiseau, depuis quelques semaines, je dis des petits mensonges et c'est ma petite soeur qui me l'a fait comprendre il y a quelques minutes ».

La maman oiseau descend de son arbre et se posa sur l'épaule du petit garçon :

« Écoutez-moi mes deux amis, aujourd'hui vous venez de découvrir qu'il faut toujours dire la vérité ; et maintenant, retournez à votre maison, il se fait tard ».

Le petit garçon remercia sa petite soeur de l'avoir cru ; ils firent tous deux un dernier au revoir à la maman oiseau et rentrèrent chez eux.

The little girl answers, "I am here and I am big; I am four years old."

Then the brother continues, "No one believed me; they all thought that I was telling a lie."

"Why do you think they thought that?" asks the mommy bird. The little boy hesitates, lowers his head and blushes with shame. "Mommy bird, in the last few weeks I have been telling small lies; it is my little sister who made me understand it a few minutes ago."

The mommy bird comes down from the tree and sits on his shoulder. "Listen, my two friends, today you have discovered that one must always tell the truth. You must now go back home; it is getting late." The little boy thanks his sister for having believed him. They say a last goodbye to the mommy bird, and return home.

Mario Auger
Né le 21 juin, 1969
Condamné pour complot et trafic de stupéfiants, 2002
Institution Leclerc, Laval, Québec

Mario Auger est né à Québec, où il grandit, le plus jeune de sept enfants. Ses parents ont divorcé quand il a eu sept ans, il a déménagé avec sa mère dans un quartier défavorisé de la ville. Il nous a décrit ses échecs scolaires et ses démèlés avec la police dès son jeune âge. Son éducation ne dépassait pas le niveau élémentaire, et il a passé son adolescence dans des foyers d'accueils. De 16 à 23 ans, il a purgé plusieures sentences dans des prisons provinciales. À l'âge de 30 ans, Mario se trouvait profondément impliqué dans une organization criminelle faisant la distribution de MDMA (Ecstasy) à l'échelle de la province. Pendant un certain temps, ses ventes de stupéfiants lui ont permis une vie stable et comfortable. Il était marié et avait deux jeunes enfants, un garçon et une fille. En 2002, Mario est arrêté et condamné pour complot et traffic de stupéfiants. Il purge sa peine à l'Institution Leclerc.

Mario a décidé de mettre à profit son temps en prison pour changer sa vie. Il est retourné à l'école, résolu à consacrer toutes ses énergies à réussir ses études. Dans les deux années qui suivirent, il passa du niveau de l'alphabétisation rudimentaire au niveau terminal de l'éducation secondaire. Ses progrès académiques éblouirent ses professeurs, et il démontre un talent remarquable pour l'écriture. Dans ses récits, Mario parle de sa vie de façon honnête et analytique. Il écrit aussi des fables et des contes ; des histoires simples et tendres pour encourager et éduquer ses enfants.

L'Institution Leclerc, un pénitencier à sécurité moyenne qui ouvrit ses portes en 1961, se trouve non loin d'une autoroute à Laval, en banlieue de Montréal, dans un champ entouré de bureaux, parcs industriels et entrepôts. Nous avons visité le pénitencier par un matin grisâtre en plein hiver. Le ciel s'est assombri au cours de la journée, et en après-midi, une tempète de neige s'est abattue sur le pénitencier et le nuit est tombée de bonne heure. Les corridors de la prison étaient sombres et impersonnels : barreaux de fer, plaques d'acier, béton et briques. Les locaux de l'école du pénitencier, pas plus modernes que le reste de l'édifice, semblent plus éclairés et moins sombres. Il en va de même pour la bibliothèque, une grande salle lambrissée en bois et décorée de vitraux, où nous avons rencontré Mario.

Mario est un homme de grande carrure, au port naturellement digne et sans prétention. Il parle peu d'anglais, et nous peu de français, de sorte que notre entrevue s'est déroulée avec le concours d'un professeur bilingue. Plusieurs des professeurs de Mario ont demandé à assister à l'entrevue. Puisque Mario n'avait pas d'objection et qu'ils étaient si fiers de leur élève, nous avons convenu qu'ils pourraient se joindre à nous. Mario a répondu à chacune de nos questions attentivement, comme s'il tenait à exprimer clairement ses idées et à bien se faire comprendre de nous.

Bien que la traduction de nos questions et de ses réponses ait ralenti considérablement l'entrevue, quand finalement elle se termina, le petit groupe d'enseignants l'applaudit spontanément, Mario accueillit cette expression d'enthousiasme avec bonne grâce, calme et humour.

Q : Tu te demandes si le fait d'exprimer tes émotions plus ouvertement signifie que tu es vraiment plus près de tes enfants ?

A : Oui... je vais avoir la réponse rien que quand ils seront plus vieux et qu'ils pourront me le dire... Ils sont jeunes, mais graduellement je leur explique que je ne veux pas être leur père, je veux être leur ami. Je veux les amener à cette idée-là, pour que, quand ils auront de la difficulté dans leurs vies, ou des situations dans leurs vies où ils auront besoin de conseils, ils seront assez à l'aise pour venir m'en parler.

Q : Ça reviens à ton histoire, « Un enfant de 7 ans ».

A : Oui, un petit peu, parce qu'il y a beaucoup de moi dans l'histoire.

Q : C'est à cause de la drogue que tu as été incarcéré. Prenais-tu de la drogue ?

A : Non. J'en avais déjà pris en masse quand j'étais plus jeune, j'ai essayé pas mal tout... Aux alentours de vingt-deux ou vingt-trois ans ma consommation était beaucoup plus forte, mais j'ai réussi à arrêter tout seul, puis c'est devenu un choix de carrière, un « business ».

Q : Parlons maintenant de ton cheminement éducatif ici. Au depart, tu pouvais a peine lire et écrire et maintenant, tu as fait énormément de progrès. Comment ça se fait ?

A : En premier, je pense que cela à commencé avant d'être arrêté parce que, quand j'ai été arrêté, quelque mois avant je m'étais inscrit à l'école. Malgré que mon commerce marchait très bien, avec tout ce qui se passait autour, je savais que, tôt ou tard, ça ne pouvait pas marcher tout le temps. Je me cherchais une alternative, et j'étais arrivé à la conclusion que je pouvais en trouver une dans les études. Mais, peut-être j'au-

rais pas eu la même motivation à l'extérieur. Je m'étais inscrit, mais peut-être que j'aurais pas persévéré... Et là on rejoint mes enfants, parce que comme individu, comme père... on parle depuis tantôt que je voulais être proche avec mes enfants et paraître à la hauteur, puis il y a toute une remise en question quand tu es arrêté, puis graduellement à venir confirmer ma première idée, que c'est à partir de l'école que j'aurai une chance de revirer ma situation de bord. Alors... j'ai pris tout l'amour que j'ai pour mes enfants, et je l'ai transformé en énergie pour réussir à l'école..., mais il ne faut pas oublier ma blonde non plus, qui y est pour beaucoup là-dedans. Elle me supporte beaucoup, elle m'encourage à vouloir changer.

Q : Quel niveau acadèmique espères-tu atteindre ?

A : Je me suis fixé le but qu'à Noël prochain, il faut que j'ai fini mon secondaire, puis s'il m'en manque, il m'en manquera en anglais... Après ça, il va me rester un an et demi à faire ici, à l'intérieur des murs, je vais commencer mon Cégep. Je vais faire sciences humaines, mais je ne peux pas dire jusqu'où je vais me rendre, parce que, pour moi, c'est un gros inconnu.

Q : On a parlé de tes plans académique. Quels sont tes plans pour ta vie quand tu sortiras ?

A : Tout est là. La question, c'est ça ! Je pourrai répondre seulement après quelques années que je serai sorti ! Pour le concret, pour l'instant, là, j'essaie de me rebâtir autour de l'école, pour me chercher une formation ou une profession qui pourrait répondre à mes besoins, mais il reste que... quand t'es en prison, c'est une réalité complètement fausse... quand j'arrive dehors, la transîtion va être dure à faire, le lien entre ce que je vais avoir développé à l'intérieur des murs, mes nouvelles attitudes, mes nouvelles manières de penser... et quand j'arrive dehors, l'ancien Mario va vouloir me dominer. C'est ça qui va

Q: You wonder whether expressing more emotions really means you are closer to your children?

A: Yes. ... I'll have the answer only when they're grown up and they can tell me themselves. ... They're young right now, but gradually I am explaining to them that I don't want to be just their father, I want to be their friend. I am trying to get them to accept this idea ... so that, when they hit a rough patch in their lives, when they are having a hard time, or when they are in a situation where they need advice, they'll be comfortable enough to come and talk to me.

Q: This relates to your story, "A Child of 7 Years."

A: Yes, there's a bit of that, because there's a lot of me in the story.

Q: It was drugs that brought you to prison. Were you using drugs yourself?

A: No. I had taken a lot of drugs when I was younger, and tried just about everything. ... At around twenty-three, twenty-four, I used a lot, but I managed to stop. And then it [selling drugs] became, really, a conscious career choice, a business.

Q: Moving forward, let's talk about the progress you have made in terms of schooling here. You started with so little ability to read and write, and have made so much progress. How did this come about?

A: First of all, I think that it started before I got arrested, because, at the time that I was arrested, a few months before that I had enrolled in school. Even though my business was going really well, with everything that was going on around me, I knew that sooner or later, something would go wrong. I was looking for an alternative, and I came to the conclusion that one place that I could find one was in school. But maybe I wouldn't have been as motivated outside. I had signed up, but maybe I wouldn't have persevered. ... And that's where we get back to my kids, because as a person, as a father ... we were talking about how I wanted to be close to my kids, and give them someone to look up to, but when you get arrested, you start to see things differently, and all this gradually confirmed my idea about school, that with school I have a chance to turn my life around. So ... I took all the love that I have for my kids, and I turned it into energy to succeed in school. ... But we can't forget my wife, either, who plays a big part in all this. She supports me a lot; she encourages me to want to change.

Q: What level of achievement do you hope you will reach?

A: My goal is that by next Christmas I will have finished high school, and if I'm missing anything, it'll be [credits for] English. ... After that, I'll have about a year and a half left here, inside, so I'll start college. I'll take the social science program, but I don't know how far I will get, because it's a real unknown for me.

Q: You've talked about your academic plans. What are your plans for when you get out?

A: That's what it's all about, that's the question! I'll only be able to answer that after I've been outside for a couple of years. For the moment, I'm trying to rebuild myself around school, to get the education or training necessary for a job that meets my needs. But ... when you're in prison, you're in a reality that is completely false. ... When I get out, it's going to be hard to make the transition between the two, to apply what I learned in here to the

arriver... Ça dépend de ta morale ! Parce que, avant ça, ma moralité était loin. Si on regarde les dernières années, mon niveau de moralité était bien bas... j'avais quelques principes de vie, mais la moralité était bien loin.

Q : Plusieurs de tes histoires traitent de la douceur, l'amitié, et de comment affronter la peur. À qui parles-tu quand tu traites de ces sujets ?

A : Principalement, c'est pour mes enfants, bien sûr. C'est sûr que là, ils sont trop jeunes pour tout comprendre ce qu'il y a d'écrit là, vraiment, malgré que mon fils puisse les lire, et pour ma petite fille, c'est sa mère qui les lit. Mais au moins, j'essaie de leur démontrer, pour plus tard, quand ils seront un petit peu plus vieux, simplement, que même si je ne suis pas là pour leur donner en contact direct l'amour et la tendresse, je peux leur en donner en écrit..., pour leur montrer une partie de qui je suis.

Q : On a été touché par tes histoires, parce qu'il semble que tu essayes d'éduquer tes enfants malgré la distance qui vous sépare.

A : Pour éclairer le premier petit point, on revient à ma mère, pour faire un parallèle..., ma mère m'a beaucoup exprimé tout l'amour qu'elle avait pour moi, donc, même s'il y avait des places où elle a eu des difficultés, ou des petits bouts qui n'ont pas marché, je ne peux pas lui en vouloir, parce qu'elle m'a tellement démontré d'amour. Alors, c'est un peu ça que j'enseigne à mes enfants.

Q : Cela nous amène à une autre de tes histoires. Dans « Le mensonge », un petit garçon demande de l'aide à sa famille, car un petit oiseau est tombé de son nid, mais personne ne le croit, sauf sa petite soeur, car il avait pris l'habitude de raconter des mensonges. Quel était ton but en écrivant cette histoire ?

A : Le but de l'histoire, c'était au service de mon petit gars, parce qu'il contait des menteries. Je voulais lui faire saisir le sens que peut-être qu'il va arriver à une situation dans sa vie, qu'il va vouloir faire une bonne action, mais les personnes ne vont pas vouloir le croire parce qu'il avait conté des petites menteries..., pour lui faire prendre conscience que ses mensonges pouvaient, peut-être, mettre la vie de quelque chose en péril.

Q: A number of your stories are about gentleness and friendship, and overcoming fears. Who are you speaking to when you talk about these things?

A: Mainly, it's for my kids, for sure. Of course, right now, they're too young to understand everything in the stories, even though my son reads by himself and my daughter gets her mom to read to her. But at least I can try to show them, for later on, when they are a little older, that even if I'm not with them now to give them love and tenderness in person, I can still give it in writing... to show them who I am, at least a little.

Q: The reason that the stories resonated for us is that it seems that you are trying to teach your children despite the distance.

A: Just to clarify the first point, it comes back to my mother, like a parallel between us. ... My mother let me know how much she loved me, a lot, so even if there were times when she had it tough, or things didn't work out, I can't blame her, because I always knew how much she loved me. So that's what I am trying to teach my kids.

Q: That leads us to the stories you wrote. In "The Lie," a little boy comes home and he tells his family that a baby bird has fallen out of its nest, and nobody believes him except his little sister, because he had been telling lies. What was your purpose with this story?

A: The goal of the story was to help my little boy, because he had started telling lies. I wanted him to realize that maybe one day he would be in a situation where he would want to do something good, but no one would believe him then, because he had told lies in the past ... that his lying could maybe even put something's life at risk.

world out there: new ways of thinking, new attitudes. ... When I get outside, the old Mario is going to want to take over, that's what's going to happen. ... It's really all a question of morality, of each individual. ... For me, before, my morality was pretty limited. If you look at the last few years, the level of my morality was really low. ... I had a couple of principles I lived by, but not really any morals.

Q : Une dernière question sur tes histories : dans l'histoire « Poilu », il y a une amitié entre un loup et un poussin. Pourquoi as-tu choisi ces animaux-là ?

A : Parce que ma petite fille a une passion pour les loups. Tu parles d'un loup, tu vas la chercher tout de suite. Elle avait beaucoup de petits problèmes à l'école – l'école, c'est la pré-maternelle – donc j'ai adapté ses difficultés dans l'histoire, pour essayer de la faire comprendre.

Q : A-t-elle encore des difficultés ?

A : Non. Des fois, en prison, on a tendance à dramatiser plus, parce que tu voudrais être là, tu voudrais aider plus, mais tu ne peux pas. Si j'étais là, il y a des choses que je pourrais leur dire ou partager plus avec eux, mais là, il faut que ce soit par les histoires que je les rejoigne. Ce qui est le plus difficile là-dedans, c'est de rentrer dans leur univers. Ils sont dans leur monde, là, surtout quand ils sont jeunes, puis, là, c'est d'arriver et de les capter, pour réussir à rentrer dans leur monde. C'est dûr à faire ! Donc, par téléphone, t'oublie ça ! Ils sont trop distraits par tout ce qui se passe dans la maison. Par l'écrit tu peux réussir un petit peu, mais c'est très, très limité.

Q : Dans ta première histoire, « Un enfant de 7 ans », tu parles d'être capable d'écrire à tes enfants pour la première fois.

A : Oui. Et personnellement, ce dont j'ai hâte, c'est de m'avancer plus dans mes études, et je me concentre bien gros là-dessus, pour quand je vais recommencer à écrire..., parce qu'il y a des choses que j'aurais voulu écrire, mais je ne trouvais pas les mots pour les écrire, pour les exprimer. Donc, là, avec plus d'études, je serai capable de m'exprimer encore plus. C'est autant pour partager avec mes enfants, mais autant, pour moi, une manière de me libérer, de faire sortir bien plus de choses que je n'arrivais jamais à dire avant.

Q : Une question de plus : ça fait deux ans que tu es ici, et tu as encore deux ans à faire. Sens-tu qu'il y a eu justice dans ce qui t'est arrivé ?

A : Il y a deux volets là-dessus, Il y a deux côtés... en calculant rapidement, sauf quelques fois où j'ai été dehors, de 16 ans à 23 ans, je les ai toutes passées en prison. J'ai grandi dans le système carcéral, plus au provincial qu'au fédéral, c'est la seule différence. Puis, il faudrait peut-être pas que je le dise, mais c'est rien que de la belle cochonnerie. Tu es fourré à mort. La seule chose qui est bonne, c'est l'école. Et je ne dis pas ça parce que les profs sont là, c'est la seule chose positive que tu peux aller chercher en quelque part. Dans mes autres sentences, je suis allé à l'école, mais j'ai jamais rien fait. J'ai souvent été sur les bancs d'école, comme il y en a ici, qui gaspillent leur temps, puis à rien faire, j'en ai fait pendant des années de temps, j'ai vécu ça bien gros. Un bon côté positif, c'est ça, parce que tant qu'au reste, c'est... Je n'ai pas vu grand monde pour qui c'était positif.

Dans le fond, c'est tellement complexe. Là c'est sûr, on doit être puni, on a fait des crimes, on a été contre la société... mais après ça ? C'est quoi la meilleure façon de réhabiliter la personne ? Je n'ai pas vraiment d'idée là-dessus. Quand je vais sortir, je vais avoir 38 ans, et en mois de faits en prison, je vais avoir dix ans de prison, et je vais avoir passé dix ans en dehors, entre 18 et 38. Donc c'est ma vie, j'ai le choix. Là, je me mets comme à égal, d'un bord comme de l'autre. Donc, l'avenir va être vraiment comme déterminant pour moi... le passé, les points comme ceux que l'on vient de mentionner, ça passe vraiment en second lieu pour moi, c'est plus ça du tout ma priorité, il faut que je passe à autre chose.

Q : Il me semble que c'est la meilleure réponse possible pour toi... et pour ta famille.

A : C'est sûr, c'est un enchaînement. **PV**

Q: One final question about the children's stories. In one, you have a friendship between a wolf and a chick. Why did you pick these particular animals?

A: Because my little girl is crazy about wolves. She just loves them. If you mention the word "wolf" you've got her attention, all of it, right away. ... I wrote it because she was having a lot of little problems at school, junior kindergarten ... so I adapted some of the things she was having trouble with in my story, to help her understand.

Q: In your first story, "A Boy of 7 Years," you talk about for the first time being able to write to your children.

A: Yes. And speaking personally, I really want to get on in school, and I'm really concentrating on that because there are things that, even if I wanted to write about them, I couldn't, because I don't have the words to write about them, or express them. So with more schooling, I'll be able to express myself even more. And, as much as it is a way for me to share something with my kids, it's also a way for me to liberate myself, to unload a lot of things that I couldn't talk about before.

Q: One further question. You have been here for several years. Do you feel there was justice in what happened to you?

A: There are two parts to that, two sides. ... If I total it up quickly, not counting a few exceptions when I was outside, I was in prison from the age of sixteen to the age of twenty-three. ... I grew up in the prison system, more in provincial than in federal, but that's the only difference. And, maybe I shouldn't say this, but it's just absolute garbage. It's crap. You're screwed all down the line. The only good thing in it is the school. I'm not saying that because the teachers are here; it's the only positive thing that you can get out of this place, and in all my other sentences I went to school, but I never did any work. I've spent a lot of time sitting at a desk in school, like some guys here, who waste their time. I've spent years in school doing nothing; I've been through that. That's pretty much it for finding a positive side, because the rest, well ... let's just say that I haven't met many people who benefited from spending time in prison.

Q: Do you think that something different should have been done when you were found guilty?

A: The whole thing is so complex, you know? Yeah, okay, we must be punished because we committed crimes; we were against society, but what then? What is the best way to rehabilitate a person? ... I don't really have any idea what to do about it. ... When I get out I will be thirty-eight years old, and if you total up all the time I've spent inside, I will have spent ten years in prison, and ten years outside, between the ages of eighteen and thirty-eight. So it's my life, I have a choice, because so far it's fifty-fifty. What happens next is really going to make the difference in my life; the next few years will determine my future. ... The past, the stuff we have been talking about, is really secondary for me; that's not my priority at all. I have to move on to something else.

Q: It sounds like the best answer you could give for yourself ... and your family.

A: Sure. It's all connected. ▣

Welcome to the Writers' Block

Matsqui Institution is a medium-security prison for male offenders, built in Abbotsford, British Columbia in 1966. Its open spaces offer beautiful views of the surrounding Fraser Valley countryside, but its grim, aging facilities leave no doubt as to its primary purpose: the secure confinement of inmates, some three hundred men in its various divisions.

Within this austere setting lies a uniquely creative island of activity: the writers' workshop conducted by Ed Griffin. Each week his group gathers at a long table in a cinderblock-walled room called "Small Social D" —otherwise known as the lifers' kitchen.

Griffin is a published novelist, but many of the significant turns his life has taken over the years can best be described with a number of "ex's": He is an ex-Catholic priest who became disillusioned with his church's lack of commitment to social justice; he is an expatriate American who immigrated to Canada out of frustration with his country's conservative shift during the Reagan era; and he is an ex-businessman, a greenhouse owner who ultimately decided he wanted to grow something more enduring than flats of annual flowers.

Griffin found his calling teaching creative writing in Canada's prison system. He has been running the writers' group at Matsqui since 1993. Griffin is a soft-spoken man whose loyalty to his students and encouragement of their creative efforts is unwavering. His students return his dedication with their spirit and focus — and with the remarkable quality of their work.

As we prepared this book, we received writing submissions from prison education programs all across the country. Many of the pieces were very good. But no single institution offered us a greater number of outstanding writers than Matsqui.

Viewed individually, each of the writings you are about to read reveals the self-reflections of a man confronting his past mistakes, his present conflicts, his future hopes and fears. As representative of the writers' group, these pieces raise questions for which we do not pretend to have adequate answers: Has Ed Griffin accidentally stumbled upon an institution that happens to be filled with inmates whose talents are unique in all of Canada? Or does the creative power he has unleashed in these men exist throughout the federal prison system, at times going unnoticed, untapped, and unrewarded?

Correctional Service
Canada

Service correctionnel
Canada

Matsqui Complex

Complexe Matsqui

Matsqui Institution
Fraser Valley Institution
Pacific Institution
Regional Treatment Centre (Pacific)
Regional Supply Depot
Community Corrections Administration
Office

Établissement Matsqui
Établissement de la vallée du Fraser
Établissement pacifique
Centre régionale de traitement (Pacifique)
Dépôt d'approvisionnement régional
Bureau de l'administration des Services
correctionnels communautaires

Canada

Ten hours in

by Jon Brown

"… You are still a young man, Mr. Brown, and I sincerely hope that you appreciate the chance you are being given today. The opportunities are there for you to get help; hopefully you take advantage of them and gain the maximum benefit from your incarceration." — Sentencing hearing, BC Supreme Court, 1995

It is funny the things you think of when you're handcuffed and shackled in the back of a van, you've just been gassed, and are waiting to be attacked by a mob of angry jail guards.

In the annals of day-to-day life, I guess it doesn't get much worse than this, but as I sit here gasping for air in a tiny four-by-four-foot cage the prominent thought rolling around in my head is, "This isn't so bad." This is my first time being sprayed and I'm amazed at how much milder it is than I anticipated. Sure, I'm a keeled-over-eyes-sealed-shut-coughing-hacking-blubbering mess who's drenched in tears and slobber, but it isn't as bad as I thought it would be.

I am a little confused as to how we got into this mess in the first place. Well, that's not entirely true, it happened so quickly that I still haven't caught back up with real time, so bear with me. My mind is moving like a dream where you're being chased and your legs are like molasses-coated corn dogs.

I find it hard to believe that ten minutes ago I was sitting in a holding cell, relatively calmly staring into a mirror, putting on my game face. My warped reflection in the grade-D plastic mirror was skewed like a smudgy crystal ball, and I definitely didn't see this moment coming.

I had been trying to psych myself up to be transferred to Matsqui Penitentiary. At twenty-one years old I had never been to the pen before, and with the exception of my brief stay here at Surrey Pre-trial Centre, some minor juvie time under my belt, and a head full of stories of what life is like behind bars, I was off to the big house. I had no skeletons in the closet; nonetheless, I was uncertain of what was to come.

I studied my face in the mirror and it was as if the image hadn't changed since I was fifteen. I was young and I looked it. I put on my "hard" face, squinting just enough to let a mean stare pierce through, then I relaxed for a few seconds before squinting again. I let out a couple of deep breaths, then made my way over to the hard plastic bench and took a seat.

The persistent hum of the fluorescent overhead lighting was making it hard to think as I scanned the cell for anything of interest. The room bore little more than a large puddle loitering around the stainless steel toilet/sink unit in the far corner of the room, a few empty paper bags and balls of wadded-up Saran Wrap sitting under the bench opposite me — the remnants of the bagged lunches that are given to the new arrivals.

Footsteps echoing through the large, sterile hallway outside the room brought me back to reality and I quickly stood and adjusted the tobacco stash that I had concealed snugly between my butt cheeks before retaking my seat. The steps grew louder and finally came to a halt at the doorway.

I turned to the window in the center of the steel door and found the face of a guard, with a slick shaved head and a dark beard, peeking in. After the airlock exuded a long hiss, the door opened and the pudgy guard approached, handing me a stack of green canvas clothing. His face spread into a thick snicker as he stepped back a few feet and said, "Okay, young man, take your reds off and change into these."

Pulling the cherry-red sweat top over my head, I wondered how many times he had repeated those same words before. Somehow, he just seemed too comfortable uttering them. Off came the red T-shirt, followed by matching sweat pants. I tried on my hard face and burned my eyes straight into his, poking sharp needles of contempt through his peepers, attempting to express my indignation. An it's-just-business look crossed his face.

I took a deep breath and pulled down my underwear, revealing my stage frightened manhood to this sexual opportunist and with grinding teeth turned to pick up the underwear off the stack of clothing he had brought in with him.

"Now, bend over and spread your cheeks," he cracked.

"What?" I snapped, turning back around to face him.

"Turn around and spread your cheeks."

"I don't think so."

He shifted his feet a couple times, then his utility belt, and then wearing his heightened face of authority he repeated himself again, adding, "Look, I'm just doing my job."

"Yeah ... no. I don't bend over for anybody." I could feel the adrenaline welling through my body, "and as for just doing your job ... in all the times I've been strip searched, I've never been asked to do that before." His blushing face told me that he knew the jig was up, that it wasn't a very good jig to begin with.

"Okay," he relented, his face souring to a deeper shade of red. "Turn around and show me the bottoms of your feet."

I turned and lifted my right foot and then my left, grabbing the underwear from the bench and pulling them on. Unable to resist the urge to try making him feel a little smaller, I turned around and gave a smug sneer, "How does it feel to be a sex offender, anyway?" I asked. In response, the heavy door slammed shut.

Five minutes later he returned and stood at the opening of the door while another guard entered and had me kneel on the bench. He manacled my ankles, then my hands were cuffed behind my back. Then I was led down the hall, through two locked doors into the sally port where a light-blue provincial corrections van was waiting. The guard opened the double doors at the back, unlocked the steel mesh cage and I hopped up into the meat wagon and took a seat on the cold bench. Metal grinded metal as the inner door slammed shut with a crunch that set my skull rattling. Yeah, I thought, the slave trade is still alive and well.

A minute later my co-accused, Joey, was brought in and silently took his place on another bench to my left. Joey was a hard case who spent most of his time in maximum security, and a fair chunk of that in the hole. I had known him since elementary school and looked to him for guidance on how to do good time. No sooner had he planted himself than he slipped his hands expertly under his legs and looped his cuffs in front of

him. I followed suit, though less elegantly, and brought the guard at the door to a full stop.

"Step back out," he said with disgust, as if we had just wasted his time. "We have to re-cuff you."

"Fuck you," muttered Joey as he settled back into his seat.

The guard's patience dwindled quickly. "Let's go!" His bellow echoed through the loading bay, while his hand reached into the cage to grab at Joey. In an instant I lunged forward and, with my cuffed appendages, smashed the guard's arm into the side of the steel wall. A wave of panic flushed his face as he pulled his arm back out and quickly slammed both sets of doors shut.

"CODE YELLOW, LOADING BAY ALPHA," the loudspeaker boomed, alerting everyone in the building of the trouble that was brewing down in the basement.

I could tell by the smile on Joey's face that he sensed the impending confrontation with the amassing mob of blue shirts surrounding the van. I didn't think that the prospect of fighting with scores of cops while cuffed and shackled was a promising idea, but Joey appeared to be thoroughly enjoying himself. He was not new to this, which is why it didn't surprise me when he made a silly attempt to reason with them, "Just get this bus on the road, you stupid pigs!" he shouted through the doors.

So you see, I know why they filled this rolling gas can with pepper spray, but the absurdity of what caused the situation in the first place is what I have a hard time grasping. There we were, handcuffed and shackled, not to mention locked in a steel cage behind two heavy steel doors. What was the big deal? Even animals in the zoo aren't as secured as we were.

What difference did it make whether our handcuffs were behind our backs or in front of us? None, so far as I was concerned, but that had become beside the point. This had quickly turned from a duel of logic to a battle of principles and, while those outside the van held very little of either in abundance, they did have the advantage of sheer numbers on their side. These were armed bureaucrats, Nazis of the modern world, and they weren't big on listening to reason. We had defied their supreme authority; we would have to be dealt with. Besides, attending a Code Yellow without some kind of confrontation is like throwing a pool party for swimming instructors and hiring a lifeguard to watch over them. It is a waste of time and training.

The guards had conferred amongst themselves for a few moments, trying to decide on a course of action. Then, after breaking from their huddle, the one standing closest to the back door opened it and asked, almost rhetorically, "Are you guys going to come out?"

A chorus of obscenities erupted from our cage. My heart accelerated and sweat began to dampen my shirt as we graciously added handfuls of dry cedar shakes to the fire mounting around us. For some reason I still held out hope that they would just drive us out of there and let the Matsqui guards deal with us on the other end. I should have known better, I should have been better prepared; I should have seen it coming. In a flash of lightning speed the inner door flew open and their assault began.

Out of the corner of my eye I caught a glimpse of Joey shielding his face with the front of his shirt, then as I began to do the same I felt the wide spray of the pepper fogger hit me on the left ear and side of my face. The initial cold shock instantly turned to a burning bumblebee burrowing into my skin. I couldn't breathe. Try as I might, I wasn't able to take in any air without succumbing to a violent coughing fit. To open my eyes was to stare into a waterfall of fire as the thick capsicum mist slowly rolled around the inside of the cage looking for any piece of skin to nestle up to and spread its love. Through the chaotic hacking I could faintly make out Joey stuttering something about not coughing, but then that was distorted by another coughing fit of my own.

A couple of minutes have passed and I've started to get my convulsions under control. I can open my eyes, if only far enough to squint through. The fits have subsided for the most part, and now are only scattered here and there, though the tears and drool are still flowing freely.

"That was the first time I've been sprayed," I confess to Joey.

"That's number twelve for me," he advises reassuringly. "Just keep breathing as slowly and deeply as you can and try not to cough."

Through the thick barrier that separates us, the sounds of the guards' coughing has superseded ours, and they don't seem to be taking it well at all. We both chuckle at the irony. Here we are, trapped inside a cage with the brunt of the blast, and it's still hitting them hard while we are relatively composed. Oh sweet, sweet justice. I'll take it where I can get it.

"Ready for round two?" Joey asks as the outer door of our cage is pulled open again. The inner door cracks and I prepare to bury my face in my shirt again, but notice a pair of blue shirtsleeves reach into our domain and grab a hold of Joey's left ankle, attempting to pull him out of the van. I immediately abandon my shirt and reached over, grabbing his right leg in a counter-attempt to pull him back in.

A tug-o-war ensues. Sides are struggling for advantage; neither is making headway, and Joey is taking the brunt of the action. I am straining to keep a firm grip on his leg as another pair of blue tentacles enters and latches on to him. His face contorts in agony as the shackles cut deep into his ankles. My grip begins to fail, so reluctantly I let go, and he is sucked through the door, swallowed by the abyss of blue and slammed forcefully onto the hard concrete. A mass of swarming guards close in on him as he struggles and kicks like a gazelle fighting off a pack of hyenas. Retractable batons strike his legs and torso as he is dragged off through the door and out of sight.

The slam of the van door lingers the way tinfoil echoes through filled teeth. Left alone in the stale metallic air of pepper and wet concrete, I try to refit my hard face, but it falters immediately. There is no one left to act hard for. I know they're coming back for me and I have to decide if I am going to come out fighting, even though I have no chance of winning, or go quietly. Hell, I don't even know if they will let me come out quietly.

Footsteps are coming back, dozens of them. I see myself leaping out of the door on top of them and taking the beating of a lifetime. It seems like the right thing to do, but I am shaking. I am five years old again, hiding under my bed, waiting for my dad to punish me. The footsteps are growing louder. Do I jump out at them or not? I don't want to have to answer now — I want more options, more time. Jesus, Joey never even stood a chance. The outer door is pulled opened.

"Are you going to come out, or do we take you out?"

I am escorted back into the cells, and I notice to my left that Joey has been strapped to a stretcher board, face down, still screaming at the world. My head falls heavy with guilt as I am moved past and into a cell. The door slams shut behind me. I have never wanted a cigarette more in my lifetime, so keeping a close watch out the window, I reach into my underwear for my tobacco stash. Oh shit. Did you know that pepper spray is a contact substance? Just my luck, that little snippet of information had eluded me until just now when the burning began to take hold of my scrotum. It came on subtly, but it is gradually gaining in intensity. The damage done, I pull out my smokes and roll an extremely loose and shabby cigarette, remove a half of a match from the package and tear off a

piece of the striker before retying the plastic baggy and putting it back into its hiding place. I light up and inhale deeply, tasting more capsicum than tobacco, then lie back on the plastic bench and listen to the myriad sounds emanating from outside. There are discussions about whether Joey can be transported while strapped to the board, but that is dismissed because the board is too long to fit into the van. There is a query to the RCMP station next door for a straightjacket.

There are steps approaching the door. I flick the smoke into the corner and sit up just as the door opens and two guards enter. One is holding a mass of chains. "Kneel on the bench," he commands.

I emerge from the cell with a new set of jewellery … belly chains, and am brought back into the loading bay and placed back into the same cage. Before long Joey is brought back into the cage, a huge smile beaming across his face, and he is sporting his own set of belly chains. He never even asks how I was taken out. His smile tells me he couldn't care less.

After a five-minute wait the van pulls out into the balmy mid-July morning and heads towards Highway 10, where we connect with the Trans-Canada and head east to Abbotsford, thirty minutes away. As an added precaution, a second escort vehicle is playing shadow at fifty feet.

We roll along the access road to Matsqui and come to a stop at a checkpoint between two twenty-foot high razor-lined fences. There is a brief conversation between our escorts and the gate guards who are checking under the hood and looking under the van with a long telescopic mirror.

The inner gate opens and we move through the fence, make a right turn, travel along the inside perimeter road, and finally come to a stop outside a nondescript door a hundred yards from the gatehouse.

The back doors open and I am seized by an entourage of ten to twelve federal guards and escorted up two narrow flights of stairs to the segregation unit. The handcuffs and shackles are removed and I am strip-searched again with no less than five guards looking on. At least this time none of them have any overt desire to view my anus. When they finish, I am given a pair of dark green coveralls and taken to one of the twenty-six cells that line the cellblock. Everything is painted baby blue.

The door is slid shut behind me and I immediately begin taking an inventory of the squalor I have been thrust into. The cell is ten feet long, seven feet wide, and about twelve feet to the ceiling. The filth is unimaginable. There is a thick crud of unknown origin spattered over nicotine-painted walls, as well as on the metal desk and on the bedposts.

The toilet in the corner makes the term "stainless steel" an oxymoron; yellowish-brown streaks are etched permanently into the steel; they ease their way down the sides of the bowl and disappear from sight into a black hole below the waterline. There are blades, obviously broken out of disposable razors, that sit perched on the windowsill; lifeless companions to the blue bed sheet that is tied into a makeshift noose and hanging eerily from the bars. An inscription has been carved deep into the blue steel door. It says, "Welcome to Ratsqui." My heart sinks. I am in a sanctuary for the suicidal, a paradise for the self-mutilator. This is to be my place of rehabilitation.

The jangling of keys turns me around to face the door and the food slot falls open with a dead thud. A commanding voice orders me to approach and place my hands through the hole and another pair of cuffs is tightly affixed. I back away and the door is unlocked and slid open.

I am led down the corridor to a shower room, which I gladly enter, and the guard slams the wire-fenced door behind me. I turn around and put my hands through the hole in the gate, but I am greeted by a look of apathy. "You'll have to keep those on," he says and walks away.

It is difficult to shower adequately with a pair of handcuffs on, but I have managed to clear most of the residual pepper spray from my skin, though I can still smell and taste the noxious substance with every breath. It takes a couple of bangs on the gate to get the guard's attention, but finally he comes and takes me back to my cell.

Upon my return I am happy to find a pile of bedding, three pouches of Export tobacco, rolling papers, and a lighter sitting on the filthy steel desk. They were obviously placed in the cell while I was taking a shower. I spread the blue sheet over the stained mattress, and then roll a smoke. I am about to lie back on the bed when a knock on the wall comes from the cell next door.

"Go to your slot." The familiar voice shoots through the wall. I pull the only moveable piece of furniture in the cell — a plastic lawn chair — over to the door and peer through the open food slot. I can see Joey's heavily tattooed arm dangling in the air. "What's up, buddy?" I call to him in greeting.

"Those goofs," he snaps, obviously aggravated, "told these pigs that they had to pepper spray us because we refused to get into the van. Can you believe that?"

"That's bullshit!"

"They're just trying to cover their ass because they know we were contained inside the van, and that they had no legal grounds to use force against us. Did you get your tobacco?" I tell him that I did and he adds with a chuckle, "They say that if we're good, we'll get a TV tomorrow. Okay, buddy, I'll see you in the yard tomorrow," he says, as his arm disappears from sight.

I pull my slot closed and walk over to the table and light my cigarette. I take a couple of drags and flick it into the toilet because it tastes too much like pepper spray. I lie down on the bed, close my eyes, and let my mind drift off as the muffled chatter of the other prisoners floats up and down the hallway.

Screams from down the hall have awakened me. I jump up off the bed and go to the door to try and see what is happening. I have no clear view and am reduced to listening to the struggle that is ensuing down by the showers. A door slams shut so forcefully the entire building shakes.

"Fuck you! You fucking goof pigs!" blasts a voice from down the hall. It is followed by a horrific smash and the sound of breaking glass and plastic. Fists are pounding off steel doors and the screams are so deafening they are causing my adrenaline to rise.

Another voice pipes up, "You're going to have to pay for that, you know," which gives rise to another tirade of violent outbursts. Pieces of what sound like a television set are being kicked around a cell, as the obscenities give way to whatever physical destruction can be managed.

After a while the range falls quiet again, and I resume my spot on the bed. My stomach is not so subtly reminding me that we haven't been fed since this morning. Hell, I don't even know what time it is.

I am jolted awake by yet more screams from down the hall, this time from the other end. Doesn't this place ever settle down? The shrieks of murder and mayhem pierce me: "Get me out of this cell!" Fists are banging off the steel door: "Hey! Get me out of here now!"

I jump up to the window in time to catch the flash of a blue shirt running past my window, the sounds of a door opening and slamming shut again, then another.

"I want a single cell right now!" a different voice is

screaming. Guards hustle past my cell, their walkie-talkies a spewing flurry of indecipherable noise. I can't see what was happening down at the end of the range, but I can make out muffled fragments of the conversation: "Holy shit, are you okay? … Don't touch him. … Yeah, it's all over the walls too. … Do you want to clean yourself up?"

After a few minutes a catatonic figure appears walking down the hall flanked by four guards who are making damn sure to keep a safe distance of several feet. Some of them are visibly gagging and trying not to vomit.

The man parading past my window is around thirty years of age. His eyes are dead and locked straight ahead, another mental casualty in the argument against double-bunking prisoners. Clad in only a pair of stained underwear, he is covered from his short-cropped blond hair to his bare feet, smeared thick like some sick primeval war paint, with his own feces.

He makes his way past my window and on towards the shower. I back away from the door, take a seat on the metal stool attached to the floor in front of the desk and roll another paper of tobacco. I wonder if he has gained the maximum benefit from his incarceration. This time I force myself to finish the whole cigarette.

I roll over onto the bed and close my eyes, pulling the pillow over my face. I try to digest the events of what has been, without a doubt, the longest day of my life.

And I've only four more years to go.

Jon Brown
Born February 16, 1974
Sentenced for robbery, 1995;
robbery with use of a
firearm, 2001
Matsqui Institution,
Abbotsford, British Columbia

Jon Brown was born and raised in Victoria, British Columbia. His parents separated when he was six, and Jon stayed with his mother. Though his family was poor, Jon says his early home life was warm and loving. He did well in school until junior high. Then he lost interest. As he describes it, he dropped out of public school, tried alternative schools, dropped out of those too. Meanwhile, he got involved in increasingly serious crimes, moving from shoplifting to breaking and entering. In 1995, when Jon was 21, he and some friends robbed a supermarket at gunpoint.

Jon was sentenced to prison for his part in this offense. He was released on parole in 1998. But he told us his plan had been to go on the run as soon as he was paroled, and that is what he did. To support himself during the next two and a half years, Jon robbed banks — by jumping over the counter and grabbing money from the teller's drawer. He committed seven such robberies before being caught. In 2001 he was returned to prison.

We met with Jon Brown in an empty classroom in the Matsqui school facility. Jon is tall; he spoke quietly, his manner restrained. Later, when we took photos first in the classroom and then while walking around the prison grounds, Jon moved extremely slowly and carefully. At last he explained he'd returned from the hospital just a few days before, where he had undergone a hernia operation. He said walking, standing, and even sitting were still causing him considerable pain.

INTERVIEW: JON BROWN

QUESTION: You've mentioned dropping out of school and getting into crime. But somewhere along the line you learned how to read and you learned how to write well. How did that happen?

BROWN: I've sort of always known how to read. Not that I really enjoyed it much, but I could read. The writing didn't come until after one of my [prison] sentences.

Q: What were the circumstances around the bank robberies?

B: Well, I got out of here in 1998 and I went on the run right away. I was pretty much set on that was what I was going to do. That's the headspace I was in. I'd talked to a bunch of bank robbers here before. They said people don't really resist when told to give you the money. Seemed like if they are not going to resist, that's going to be better for everyone. Easier … although it wasn't much money. It was hardly worth it. I got away with it for two and a half years. ... I got away with seven of them. And then on the last one, just bad luck, there happened to be a cop right there.

Q: When we showed the writing that we were thinking of putting into the book to the prison authorities, there were a few pieces they expressed concern about. Yours was one of them … specifically your description of the strip search.

B: They probably didn't like the allusion to a sex offender. But if you look at the act, instead of looking at who's doing it, when they tell you to take off your clothes and bend over, that [feels like] sexual assault. ... Yeah, they have security issues. But if you look at the act, what is going on, it's really not that much different.

Q: Do you feel you're different now from the person in your story?

B: Definitely different. At the time of the story, I was twenty-one years old. ... Honestly I was nervous coming to the penitentiary. I was trying to find a way to fit in. ... I had to really put on a front. I went through a span of years, my whole last sentence, keeping that front up. ... Arguing with the guards, not doing any programs, not doing anything. And that was a defense mechanism, too, to establish a name or whatever.

Q: At the beginning of your story, you talk about your fear.

B: Which is something I would have never admitted at the time. ... Yeah, I was worried about coming to jail.

Q: You're potentially out in under a year. What are your plans?

B: Two years of parole. I know the reality of that. If you want to stay out, you basically have to keep parole, do what you're told. So while I'm going to be out, I'm not really planning on being too mobile or anything for a couple years. Like I say, I wasted most of my childhood. ... There are some things I've got to straighten out. ... Last time when I was here I didn't do any programs or anything. I didn't really even contemplate why I was here. So when I got out, I was like, Screw them, I'm going to be a better robber this time. I think the motivation was to show that I can be good at something. Even if it was the wrong thing to be good at. ... I was sort of the moral thief. I would be very polite, please and thank you. ... I made myself feel better about [what I was doing]. It wasn't my intention to go in and scare people, terrorize people. I just wanted the money. ... It sounds absurd, but I got the "Gentleman Robber" handle from the papers.

Q: Your request to be moved to a lower security prison was denied a while back. What was the reason?

B: One of the things they are concerned about is that I can't verbalize my crime cycle. So they wanted me to work one-on-one with a psychologist to work through this.

Q: What is your crime cycle?

B: I sort of saw myself as a Robin Hood. But not really, because I wasn't giving to anybody, I was keeping it for myself. That's what it was, getting back at society for being so cruel, but really I was contributing to it, I was sort of doing the same thing. ... Maybe I felt, well, if I had money or things, that I would feel better about myself, or my anxiety, people would like me better. So I'd go and steal for it, and it never really helped. I felt worse.

Q: How much was drug use an issue during your robberies?

B: Oh no, it wasn't for drugs. The first robbery, they made a pretty big deal of it, that there was cocaine. We'd done coke for about a week prior, but it wasn't like we were doing it all day every day ... that became more of an excuse in court. ... I still smoke pot but maybe it's once a month or once every couple of months, very infrequent. I just don't function well on it anymore. ... I used to smoke it every day. Now, I can take very little of that. But as far as the bank robberies, drugs weren't an issue at all.

Q: I'm surprised.

B: So are most people actually. ... Which is something I think concerns the CSC [Correctional Service Canada] too, because at least with drugs they sort of know why. But when it's not drugs involved, it's sort of, You did that when you were straight? ... That's going to be hard for them to accept. But that's the reality of it. ⊠

Five Bucks'll Getcha Burned

by Mike Oulton

The loud stinging buzz of my cell door woke me up at seven a.m. The sound of all thirty doors buzzing open at once was like a pack of motorcycles on the highway. I slumbered down to the kitchen for breakfast, still half asleep, and sat down at the table where I met Justin. The seat was mine, and with the comfort came responsibility and an added chance of drama.

Breakfast would be the same every morning, Justin said — French toast or pancakes. The menu never changed. I guessed it was the jail's way of making sure we went completely insane. I learned later that the worst thing about the meals in the dining room was that they never came at the temperature they were supposed to be eaten. The cold plates came warm and the hot meals always arrived cold, even if they just came out of the oven. After a while I got used to it.

When I returned to the living unit, I grabbed a broom and a mop bucket full of bleach and water. The night before I had rolled over and touched a sticky nicotine patch on the wall with enough residue to satisfy ten smokers. Needless to say, I still felt dirty living in that cell. Ten years was a lot of time to spend avoiding nicotine spots. The entire room needed one last scrub.

On my way down the hall, the door to the cell beside mine buzzed open. A lanky figure slunk out of his cell and down the hallway towards me. His dirty blond shoulder-length hair fanned out across his back. He had a towel in his hand. A collage of tattoos covered one whole arm; the other arm was bare. I stood up straight and prepared myself for another undesired encounter with one of many freak shows that walked the halls in prison. For some reason, I hadn't seen my

neighbour until that moment. I assumed that he was a junkie and had been comatose on heroin for the last few days.

"You new?" he said. Thank God he never offered his hand.

I nodded and glanced at the floor like everyone did in this place. It was a reaction that he could relate to. I didn't get a good vibe from him. He seemed nervous and the tone of his few words was rugged. He walked right by me without saying another word. He must have been a mind reader, because he walked right into the shower at the end of the hall.

Twenty minutes later I stood outside my cell looking at the shiny walls and floor. The nicotine stain beside my bed was gone, along with most of the paint. I was glad that I didn't smoke. Nicotine tears still dripped down the wall even after I'd already scrubbed them bare. I could only imagine what a smoker's lungs looked like. I was about to do a final mop when the hairball from the shower reappeared at my doorway. He leaned into my freshly scrubbed cell and inhaled.

"Smells pretty good," he said. "Better than the last guy."

Better than you, I thought. A snarl appeared on his face when I didn't answer. I'd met plenty of people in my life that walked around with scowls on their faces, but this guy's glare was so mean it made you want to slap your mother. Most people didn't want to be mean, they just wanted to make an impression that they weren't weak.

right next door to me. His screams replayed over and over in my head. The smell of burning hair lingered in the air around me.

"Hey."

I looked up to see a young Oriental con at my door. I stood up, ready for anything. "That was pretty brutal, eh?"

I exhaled a lung full of nervous air. "Yeah."

"You should've just let it go. He had that coming to him. He owed money."

I rubbed my face with both hands, trying to shake the disbelief from my eyes.

"What? Really? How much?"

The con shrugged. "Not much. Something like five bucks. Don't matter though. Five, ten -— it'll all getcha burned, man."

Five bucks will get you burned. Five bucks will get you lit on fire in the penitentiary. The day before when the guy asked to borrow money from me, I had said no. I rejected his plea for help. I didn't even know his name. He got burned. Was it my fault? If only I would have put aside my pride, done something good for once and lent him the money, would he have been here today? If I did lend the bale of tobacco to him, what if he didn't pay me? Would I have to light him up? I wasn't prepared to do something like that. I didn't have the nerve.

"You better watch out," said the Oriental kid. He stepped out of my doorway and lit a cigarette. My eyes widened at the sight of the flame. "The guys that put out the hit are going to be upset that you helped him. You should've just let him burn."

Ten years of this? I couldn't imagine what more there was to see. I'd never been that close to death in my life. I made a promise that I'd never do anything to get myself involved in a situation that could possibly get me lit on fire. You should've just let him burn. Up to that point in my life, it was the most powerful statement I'd ever heard.

Mike Oulton was born and raised in Victoria, British Columbia. Trouble came early to him: Mike says he was shoplifting by the age of nine, and was a problem student throughout grade school. His mother and stepfather were unable to control him on the streets or in the classroom. By the age of eleven Mike was placed in a residential behavioral program at a psychiatric hospital in Victoria. Later he was sent to live in foster care.

Mike says he started dealing drugs when he was about seventeen — and he began a relationship with an older woman who was also a drug dealer. As Mike moved deeper into the drug world over the next decade, his earlier pattern of petty crime declined. Still, he estimates he's spent ten of the last fifteen years in prisons in Canada and the U.S. Eventually he was arrested in Mexico for cocaine trafficking. He spent over a year in a Mexican jail and was then allowed to finish his sentence in Canada. In 2001 he was sent to Matsqui Institution.

Mike had started writing a journal in Mexico. However his real commitment to writing began in Matsqui, and flourished in Ed Griffin's writers' workshop. Today Mike writes prolifically, producing well-crafted short stories, novels, and screenplays. His writing style is direct, polished, and confident. He writes both on his own and in collaboration with Ed.

We met with Mike Oulton on the first day of our two-day visit to Matsqui, in the dark, heavy, stone and steel building that houses the institution's school. Mike has a room-filling personality — his voice is resonant; he is upbeat and outgoing; he joked confidently with us. After our interview in the classroom, we went outside to take photos of him on the prison grounds. The day was cool, windy and sunny. Mike Oulton seemed far more in his element on Matsqui's wide grassy field under an open blue sky than he had in the prison's claustrophobic school building.

Mike Oulton
Born July 18, 1975
Sentenced for possession
of schedule I/II substances
for the purpose of trafficking;
trafficking in narcotics, 2001
Matsqui Institution,
Abbotsford, British Columbia

Q: What is your crime cycle?

O: Feeling sorry for myself. Feeling sorry I was in a foster home, feeling sorry I couldn't make friends, that kind of thing. Crime was the only place that I could go that really accepted me. It didn't matter where you came from, what you did, what you looked like. If you were making money, you were accepted and people wanted to be around you. For me a lot of it was greed. ... The money was just too, too easy; it was way too easy and it allowed me to live the lifestyle that I wanted. I think, now as a twenty-nine-year-old man, there are more important things. ... It's a crime cycle but it's also a growing cycle. The crime cycle is part of some people's growing cycle and sometimes you need to go though that kind of thing to know who you are, what you're all about.

Q: You feel like you've grown out of it?

O: You know what? I think that I've matured in it.

Q: Part of your dream is to be a writer. But you're choosing a profession that is all about dealing with rejection.

O: Yes, it is. I'm not really scared of that.

Q: What's your goal as a writer?

O: I want to entertain. I love to make people laugh. I want to make people think. ... I want to be the type of guy that writes funny stuff and then turns around and hits somebody with something very dramatic or life changing.

Q: When we were talking before, you said there were three important things for surviving in prison. One is staying healthy, working out and so on. The second is improving yourself. And the third one?

O: Spirituality. Your health is one thing; doing school work or learning, that's important, that makes you a different person as well. And your spirituality, I mean it's so important to believe in something. It doesn't always necessarily have to be God or Allah or Buddha or whatever, but believing in something. It is so important because it creates inner peace. ... I know where my calling is and my calling really is to entertain people. If I can entertain people, if I can teach people, if I can do something like that, I'm getting through to my goals. My dreams are becoming reality. And that's what life is about. ▣

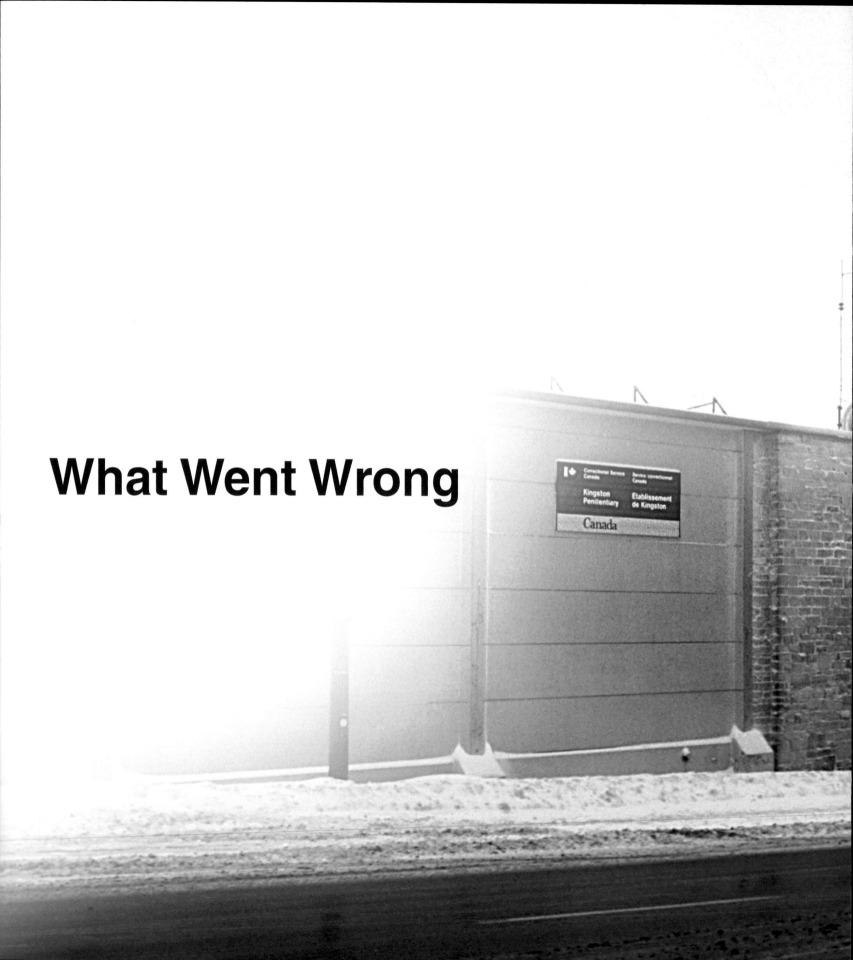

What Went Wrong

I was born in Kingston, Jamaica. My mother and father were newlyweds, and I was their first child. My sister Georgia was born two years later. I cannot remember very much about my early childhood. I do remember that we lived in a house on a beautiful beach where my father liked to take me for walks in the sand and play with me in the water. By the time I was four years old, for reasons I did not know, my mother decided to leave Jamaica. Many young women left Jamaica in those days to try and make a better life for themselves in Canada, England, or in the United States, but I know that was not necessary for my mother to do. My father had just started his own business, and both my mother and father were from very wealthy families. In her decision to leave Jamaica, my sister and I were brought to the home of my mother's parents.

My grandparents lived in the parish of Trewlany, in a town called Albert's Town. It's a farming town which produces a lot of yams and bananas. My grandfather was one of the wealthiest men in the whole parish. He had several yam plantations. He also had banana plantations, and he had many men and women who worked the fields for him. We lived in a very large and beautiful house. The house had a total of ten bedrooms. We had orange trees, mango trees, tangerines, and apple trees all in and around the huge yard. We also had many animals such as horses, donkeys, dogs, pigs, chickens, and pigeons close by our house.

Because our town was so small, we had two schools, a primary school and a secondary school. We had to have teachers come in from other parishes to teach in our schools. My grandparents made an agreement with the board of education to provide housing for some of the teachers who came to our town. So we usually had five or six teachers living at our house during the school months. My grandmother had local women working with her to wash their clothes and do other duties.

That was the environment I grew up in. I've missed it since the day my mother came back to Jamaica when I was twelve years old and brought me to Canada. I did not know my mother until that year when she decided she wanted to be a "mommy." My grandparents were mother and father as far as I was concerned. I just remember getting Christmas or birthday cards (with a $20.00 bill) that said "Love, Mom." And even though my father was in Jamaica, I hardly ever saw him. But I didn't feel in any way neglected because we had everything we needed and more. My sister and I were loved very much by our grandparents and I was already being groomed to take over all my grandfather's plantations.

I would have to go to the fields with the workers during holidays and I was taught various things about planting and harvesting yams and bananas. I would also help to load the trucks to take the yams and bananas to the markets and other distributors. Sometimes I would go with my grandfather in his truck to deliver to other parishes such as Saint Ann, Saint Mary, Spanish Town, or to Jamaica's capital city, Kingston. These were my favourite times. They were the happiest times of my life. When I wasn't doing things with my grandfather I spent my free time with my friends going fishing, hunting birds, or trapping crawfish which we would cook and eat. We also played cricket or soccer. Our lives were so uncomplicated.

Then it all changed for my sister and me. I know it all changed for my grandparents a lot too when my mother suddenly came back to Jamaica and announced that she was taking us away. For the month that my mother spent in Jamaica making the final arrangements to take us away, I saw my grandparents in a way that I had never seen them before. My grandmother became very quiet and my grandfather and my mother were always arguing. My sister was scared to leave our grandparents and as for me, I just didn't want to leave period. And I was sure that my grandfather would make sure I wouldn't have to leave. Why should I have to leave all my friends and most of all why should I have to leave my "Mama" and "Papa" to go with someone I didn't know and now someone I didn't like because she was trying to force me to leave the home I was so happy in.

But my mother was convinced that Canada was the best place for us. She was now a dietician and she wanted her children in Canada with her. And that's all she had to say on that matter.

Finally the day came for me to be forced to leave my grandparents and my home. We had a party at the house the night before. There were a lot of people there to see us off. My mother and grandfather got into a very loud argument. He was still trying to change her mind. Anyway, the next day we were in Montego Bay at the airport.

Something happened that day at the airport that I will never forget for the rest of my life. My grandfather broke down and cried like a child. There was never another time that I saw him like that. He wouldn't let me go, and we were both crying. He asked my mother to take my sister, and said that she should leave me with him. But she said no.

Recently, I was sitting in my cell in Millhaven Reception and I thought of how distraught my grandfather was that day. It's as if he knew how my life would turn out if I left Jamaica at that time. I know my mother was just trying to give me and my sister a better opportunity to get a good education and a career here in Canada. Every mother has the right to seek out the best for her children, and her plan worked very well for my sister. My sister is very successful. She is an executive with Revenue Canada. She is married with three beautiful children and lives in the suburbs.

But things didn't work out that way for me. From the beginning, things started to go wrong. First of all at home with my mother. From the very beginning my mother's expectations were far too great for me. She expected me to be perfect. I didn't ever get a chance to adjust properly.

My mother was a perfectionist. There was no room for any mistakes or failures in her world. So as a result my sister and I were handled with very strict discipline. We were expected to be model children for Mommy. That way, she could show us off to her friends and co-workers. That was impossible for us. We had just arrived in Canada. How could we compare with her friends' kids? How could we get perfect marks in school? We were coming from a home in Jamaica where there was so much love and patience. There was no pressure on us to be perfect. We were being raised gradually, but not without the necessary discipline that children need. But what my mother was doing was wrong. I guess in her mind she thought she was doing the right thing. But to me she was just being cruel.

There was just too much mental and physical abuse. If I ate one cookie more than what was left out for us, I would get a beating. If I didn't clean my room perfectly, I could get a beating or yelled at for the whole day. If I didn't get good marks in school, I was slapped and for a week would be yelled at about how stupid and good-for-nothing I was. I remember countless days and nights when I would cry in my room for my grandparents. I was afraid of this woman whom I only knew for two years and who was supposed to be my mother. It was like a nightmare. Why was I taken from my loving home? Why didn't my mother like me?

By the time I was fifteen years old, I honestly think I hated my mother (God forgive me!) That's when my rebellion began. I eventually left home when was seventeen years old. The last twenty years of my life have been a complete disaster. But my greatest accomplishments have been my children. I have not always been there for them, but they know I love them because I always tell them so. And they love me too.

It has taken a lot of time in jails and a lot of suffering to finally come to terms with myself. But I'm finally at peace with myself. I now pray to God for forgiveness for my past lifestyle of drugs, crime, and sin in general. I have forgiven my mother.

You know, it's ironic. But it seems that she was really trying to save me from what she unknowingly pushed me into twenty years ago. Life can be complicated and even unfair. But I don't have the time to feel sorry for myself anymore. I must now trust my belief in God to give me the courage to change my life. I look at my past as the first stage of my journey in life. So I must learn from my mistakes and move on.

I also feel an obligation to use my experiences for good in the future, first with my own children, but also to help the youth out there who are heading in the same direction as I went. I plan to volunteer with organizations that work with troubled youth when I get out of prison. I know I have a lot to offer in that area. I believe that is part of God's purpose for me. Maybe that's why I had to suffer for so long trying to find myself. In the Book of

Galatians 5:22-23, it says, "The fruits of the spirit include long suffering." This and other verses have helped me to know peace with myself. I believe that all the suffering I've gone through in life was to make me a better person. I can use all the badness for good in my future. I cannot sit around and wonder what went wrong. To be totally honest, it doesn't really matter. What really matters to me now is to make sure there's no more wrongs. I have the rest of my life ahead of me to do right. My grandparents both died while I was in jail. And I know they loved me to the end.

So now I know exactly how I want to live. Now I'm dedicating my future to my Mama and Papa. I will rejoice in hope; and be patient in tribulation.

Thank you for loving me. Rest in Peace.

We met with **Orville Young** in the Kingston Penitentiary library on a snowy January mid-morning and decided to do our photography session with him before sitting down for our interview. As picture-taking began, Mr. Young confessed to feeling self-conscious about a wound on the inside of his upper lip. He wondered how it would appear in pictures. The wound, which turned out to be an old scar, was not visible to us and we told him so.

Kingston is a maximum security institution. Its massive cut-stone buildings and claustrophobic corridors reflect unblinking attention to the containment and control of the people it holds. Outside of the prison library, our range of photo locations was limited to a small stretch of corridor between the locked steel door to the yard and the first barred gateway leading into the cellblocks. We needed to stop shooting at one point while corrections officers escorted several inmates through the hallway in chains.

Mr. Young is a big man, muscular and imposing, but his facial expression and the general way he carries himself suggest sadness and somber thoughtfulness. His voice is deep; he speaks softly, and with a calm, almost courtly politeness. Mr. Young started the interview by reading "What Went Wrong." He read slowly and deliberately. As his reading went on, Mr. Young struggled to hold back his tears. When the task was finished, he took a few minutes to get a drink of water and compose himself. Then we began our questions.

Orville Young
Born July 25, 1964
Sentenced for robbery, 2001
Kingston Penitentiary,
Kingston, Ontario

Q: You say that you see your past ... these are your words ... as "the first stage of my journey in life." When did that stage end?

Y: I couldn't say it's just one day ... it's been gradual, coming to this stage. Maybe it's just age. Even though I'm thirty-nine years old, up until recently I didn t feel that way. Because I've missed out on my whole childhood. Like it's been a blur. Getting your driver's license ... all the little things ... going on your first little date ... that just didn't happen in my life. ...

Q: You're out of here in a relatively short time.

Y: Ten months.

Q: How are you different now?

Y: I feel different, I think different. And I think it's just like ... I have the opportunity now to be different. There's no reason why I shouldn't. Even the fact that I don't have to look over my shoulder anymore.

Q: Have you always been religious? When did you become more connected?

Y: Religious is not probably what I am. I'm not a church fanatic. I just think it's spirituality. It's a genuine belief in my heart, in God. It's not a belief in God like I have to run around and go to church every Sunday and walk around with a Bible in my hand and try to force my beliefs onto everybody. It's like a one-on-one thing between me and God, in my heart.

Q: In your piece you say that you "feel an obligation to use my experience for good in the future." How are you going to do that?

Y: The first thing I want to do, I want to volunteer to work with any organization out there, John Howard, any organization out there that's willing to give me the chance to volunteer when I get out. I will be going from here to a CSC halfway house. And again that's perfect in my plan. It's going to help me gradually. Any organization out there that's working with youth as far as prevention, youth rehabilitation, youth awareness. Any organization like that in the community that's willing to give me the opportunity to sit down and talk to kids. I particularly want to work with kids.

Q: Getting back to the spiritual aspect that you were talking about before, how does that balance with the day-to-day stresses of being in here?

Y: It actually balances really good. I have no problems. None. That's with guards, with inmates, none. If I walk down the hall I get along with everybody. I'm kind of like known as a peacekeeper as far as that's concerned. Guys come to talk to me, guys if they need to borrow a pack of cigarettes on my range. ... I don't side with Blacks ... I'm just in the middle and everybody knows that. I think everybody respects me for that. I'm doing the easiest time I've ever done, and that's pretty unusual for this place, because this place has a reputation, but again it's just more testament, I think, to what's really going on.

Q: You're doing your own time?

Y: Doing my own time and doing whatever I can to help anybody else do their time too. ... I just feel like a good guy. I want to be a good guy. Know what I'm saying? I don't let nothing bother me. If someone does something I don't like, whereas before it would be like the attitude ... I'm not like that anymore. I'll be like ... maybe you shouldn't have done that, maybe you shouldn't have said that. I'm happy with it. I feel good. ... Now I'm just ... everything's there. I have all the tools now. Now it's just I want to get out and put everything into action and just watch it grow. I'm so anxious, I'm so excited that I know I'm not going to fail. Doesn't mean I'm just going to come out and ... I know I'm going to have to work at it, I know I'm going to have to do what's necessary. But I'm confident

Broken Wings

Sometimes the darkness
seems to be my light in these dreadful days,
my mind races, yet the demons still stay.

I want to run but it'll follow me,
I long for freedom,
but it's complete darkness; I can't see.

Where did my dreams go?
They're so untouchable now.

I've always wanted a family,
and a man who'd cherish my vows.
I looked forward to teaching my grandchildren
about life's mysteries,
But all I have now is insanity and complete misery,
endless heartache.

The tears overflow.
I was once a beautiful woman inside,
but now my heart has lost its glow.

rebecca reid

My name is Rebecca Reid. I am serving my second federal sentence for armed robbery. I am the oldest of three children. I have a sister who is thirty, and a brother aged twenty-six. All three children have different fathers. When I was ten years old, my brother's father took my brother away and I didn't see him for years.

My mother was addicted to Valium and alcohol. I can remember my mom being on the couch, her eyes in the back of her head. My sister's father was there. I remember an ambulance taking my mom away, and that was the last time I saw my sister: My sister lived with her father from there on.

I did not know my father when I was very young. He was struggling with his addictions to alcohol and speed. I first met him when I was ten years old at my grandmother's place in Toronto. I remember this because my father couldn't stop kissing and hugging me, and I remember feeling uncomfortable with it. I sensed that my mother was trying to get me to live with my father because she was progressing in her addiction. As a result of losing my brother and sister, combined with my mother's addiction, I started acting out and running away from home. My mother put me in foster care and I still ran away, until the social worker and my mom agreed to have me placed in a psychiatric facility for six months. After that, I was placed in another foster home ... and I ran away again.

During this time I smoked my first joint and had my first beer. When I was fourteen years old I got in an argument with my mother and the argument resulted in a physical fight. My mother charged me with assault and I was sentenced to serve a year in an open-custody group home. While in the group home I remember going to a friend's house to buy hash, and witnessing intravenous drug use. I was shocked and curious at the same time. Instead of buying hash, I injected twenty-eight units of speed into my arm.

By the age of sixteen I was on the streets hanging with all my friends. I was introduced to cocaine and heroin, and I first solicited to support my lifestyle. I was still sixteen, and using cocaine every day, when I found out I was four months pregnant. I remember going to the doctor's to get an abortion, but the doctor scared me with the details and I ran out.

My son Nathan was born on December 7, 1988, addicted to cocaine. To this day he is challenged because of my drug use. I haven't seen him since he was in diapers. I don't think I can ever forgive myself for what I did to my son. I will take this pain to the grave. In total, I have three boys. My second son, Cody, is adopted and living in Richmond, British Columbia. My youngest son, Chance, is three years old. He lives in Toronto with my Aunt Judy. Losing your children because of your drug addiction ... this pain has to be the worst.

I have lived in Vancouver, Calgary, Edmonton, Saskatoon — I was a drifter in my addiction. In 1997, I was convicted of armed robbery and served three years in Edmonton Institution for Women. I married while I was incarcerated, to a man who was serving time in Edmonton Maximum Institution. On November 13, 1999, I was married in a maximum-security penitentiary and all the guests were members of a gang called Alberta Warriors. We had a seventy-two-hour private family visit and this is when our son, Chance, was conceived.

I had been paroled, and one of the stipulations of my parole was to reside under my mother's supervision. I hadn't really lived at home since the age of ten, being in foster care. Living with my mother on parole, being pregnant, trying to remain clean, was hell. When I had my son, I had to fight to take him home. With the stress of my mother, parole, and feeling like I was under the microscope, I ended up using again.

My son lives with my aunt now. He calls her Mom and me, "Auntie Becca." While I was relapsing, I was raped by a man who held a knife to my neck and demanded sex. A few months later I found out I was HIV-positive. I guess I am still in the stages of grief. There are some days when I can keep my head up and I tell myself to be strong, but the reality of the feelings inside comes through when my cell door shuts and I am left alone to think, to cry, to try to tell myself I have survived many things and I can survive this as well.

I hooked up with the AIDS Committee of Guelph, and I was asked to sit on the Board of Directors. I am also on the Speakers' Bureau. I have spoken several times to tell my life story. I have built a good support system since I was diagnosed with HIV. I have gotten much closer to my support worker, Tom, in this past year. He gives me strength and hope. He shows me how to see a glimmer of light even when the world seems totally dark and I'm all alone facing this death sentence.

Rebecca Reid
Born December 31, 1970
Sentenced for robbery, 2003
Grand Valley Institution for Women,
Kitchener, Ontario

Rebecca Reid's writings about her life describe a journey to personal destruction — from her troubled childhood in a fragmented family, to drug addiction, prostitution, and crime in her early teens through her twenties, to her discovery when she was 31 that she was infected with the AIDS virus. There were other similar stories among the manuscripts we received, but Rebecca's reaction to what she has called "this death sentence" of HIV infection was uncommon. She writes of friends who actually increased their self-destructive behaviour once they found they were HIV-positive. When Rebecca received her diagnosis, she decided instead to take control of her life. Her writing ends on a strong note of hope.

Grand Valley Institution for Women is a medium/minimum security prison. Established in 1997, it currently houses over 80 inmates. We met Rebecca in an open, sunlit lounge area overlooking a snow-covered garden. She wore simple make-up and was tastefully dressed in decidedly non-institutional clothes. The teacher who introduced us confided Rebecca had put considerable effort into preparing for our visit.

As our interview went on we found ourselves surprised by aspects of Rebecca's personality that were missing from her writing but which quickly revealed themselves as we spoke: her cheerfulness, her enthusiasm, her self-effacing sense of humour. We took photographs both in the wintry garden and at various spots around the institution. Then we went into one of the classrooms to conduct our interview, and Rebecca spoke candidly about her past experiences, her present outlook, and her plans for the future.

INTERVIEW: REBECCA REID

QUESTION: What was your reason for wanting to write your story?

REID: For my children. Because I have HIV ... so when they are older they will be able to understand. Instead of hearing from other family members, I want them to know that this comes right from me, and this is what I went through in my life.

Q: Have you experienced any AIDS symptoms?

R: No. I'm not on any medication for HIV because my immune system [is] still normal.

Q: You've said you're a drug addict. What drugs are you addicted to?

R: I'm a heroin and crack cocaine addict.

Q: Can you see the possibility of not using?

R: No. I've tried and I've tried. I've been using hard drugs since I was fourteen years old. I've been in so many treatment centers. Part of understanding myself is accepting that if I want to binge once in a while, I will. I still want a job, I still want to work at an AIDS organization. I still want to do good things in my life. I want to stop doing robberies. I want to stop coming to jail. But I believe for the rest of my life there will be a time that I will be high once in a while. And that is just accepting me.

Q: And yet in your writing you say that you feel you've come to a new level.

R: A new level in terms of my HIV, a new level in accepting myself. I've always tried and tried to stay clean. I've gotten on such a high pedestal, and every time I've fallen, and I'm just sick and tired of trying and trying and

falling flat on my face. ... So if I stop putting those expectations on myself and just live my life day by day, without drugs ... I'm not going to tell myself that I'm never going to use again. That's where I'm at right now. I can say to myself, I don't have to be working the streets, I don't have to be doing robberies ... doing all this stuff to support my habit. I don't want to be that way. Once in a while I'll get high and then leave it alone. But that's not crack cocaine. If I use crack cocaine I'm gone. I'm just talking about doing a little bit of heroin for one night. ... I can honestly say that I do not want to use crack cocaine again. I know that drug is evil.

Q: You mention starting to run away at age twelve.
R: I was really resentful of my mom because she gave up my brother and my sister. We were all once living in a nice townhouse. I remember my step-dad one day coming in and taking my brother away. I didn't know he was my step-dad, I called him Dad. I didn't understand he wasn't taking me too, he was just taking my brother. I remember hanging off of his leg. He moved out my brother's furniture and that was that.

Q: How old were you at that point?
R: I was nine. ... I went from living in a townhouse to living in a total dump. We had no sheets on the bed. My mom was really actively drinking. Parties all the time. I started drinking too, to the point of blackout. I was only about eleven then.

Q: How did you learn to write?
R: I was always good in English in school. I don't really know [why]. My mom and my grandmother write poetry too. My mom used to write some pretty sad stuff, while she was drinking. I used to read that. I can write poetry when I'm really down.

Q: Have you had contact with your mom recently?
R: Yeah. My mom has been clean for fourteen years. She's straightened up. She's a personal support worker. She's changed her life around. It's a whole new mom. When I left years ago, my mom was still drinking and doing pills. I had gone out west, and then I came back in 2000 and I was like, who the hell are you? [Laughs] I hadn't lived at home since age ten with my mom. It was very hard for me to be pregnant [with her youngest child], taking my stat release to Ontario, having the baby there, having the baby taken away by Children's Aid, having my family step in. Being on parole. It was nuts. I was under the microscope because my mother still had this image of me from years ago — how bad of an addict I was back then when I was in my teens. I was really bad. Now I'm a binge user. I can clean up for a year or two. I have more sobriety time than mess-up time.

Q: Do you have any contact with your oldest son?
R: No. He's fourteen, and I've got to wait until he is eighteen.

Q: And your middle son?
R: I have letter and picture contact with Cody. He's adopted. They've told him that he has a real mom. But they are going to wait until he's a little bit older to read him my letters. I've made him books. All the time I'm sending him pictures of my family. Of my children and stuff like that. ... He's ten. I get letters from [his adoptive mother]. She tells me how he's doing and sends me pictures.

Q: What's your relationship like with your youngest son?

R: Since my aunt has him, she's really taken over. He calls her Mom, and that used to really bother me at first — to the point that I couldn't even really see my son. I couldn't handle it. I'm at the point now that I'm happy he's in my life, that he's in my family's life. My mom can spend time with him and take him for weekends. Because she's never really had any grandchildren around her, I'm really glad that they have that. He looks just like me. Spitting image. ... My husband's never met him. My husband is still incarcerated.

Q: Let's talk about that relationship. How did you meet your husband?

R: Honestly? [laughs] There was a big crack house in Calgary. I used to see him there and then we lost touch with each other. We found each other again when we were both in prison. We started writing. And that's how we got married.

Q: Your correspondence in prison is what led to you being married?

R: He'd asked me before, when we were on the streets together. But I never accepted.

Q: The whole time of your marriage he's been in prison?

R: I've had two PFVs [private family visits] with him and I've had my husband out of prison for a month. I got us a little apartment. I was four months pregnant. And that's the extent of my marriage.

Q: How did the two of you get along outside of prison?

R: It was very hard, because I'm used to doing my own thing when I'm using. I'm not used to having a man. It was very hard to stop myself from going out on the street and making money and stuff like that. So we had to do other things together to get money.

Q: What kinds of things?

R: Robberies.

Q: What have been the best times of your relationship?

R: When he's in prison [laughs]. I don't really think it's such a bad idea. He can be in prison for as long as he wants. I can visit him and have PFVs, but still have my little domain outside.

Q: Let's get to your plans for when you get out of prison. What would you like to do?

R: I've already done some speaking engagements at the University of Guelph. I spoke in front of 250 people. I told my life story. That was about two years ago. And I spoke at treatment centers ... in front of drug counsellors, doctors, and social workers. I'd like to work in a group home like I was in, to work with youth. I'd like to be a social worker someday. I'm in school right now trying to get my grade twelve. ... I never really learned in school. High school was one big party.

Q: You've made it clear you're making steps to change your life. Where are you in terms of steps forward and steps back?

R: I'm in a methadone program, because I'm really trying to stay off drugs. ... I want to be on it for when I get released, as a stepping stone to help me cope with being out there. ... Being off the methadone program and thinking I could do it on my own ... that would be a major step backwards, because I can't. I've tried endlessly, and I just keep screwing up. I hate it; it's very hard on me.

Q: You've written about your inner child. The image of the little one inside you ... where did that image come from?

R: When I was a little girl, I had really long brown hair, and I remember seeing pictures of myself. I was wearing a little blue dress, and I was holding a peacock feather in my hand. That time, that's when I was whole. That's when I wasn't abused. ... I wasn't going through all the stuff my mom put me through. I was still little Becky. I believe it's her, the little Becky, who has been watching over me. Because I was okay at one time. It's the young one that I was that is taking care of me. That's who I pray to, that's who I ask help from. I believe in angels. There are angels everywhere. This story I wrote is just a small part of my life. I've been through so much more. And I'm still here today. Yeah I got HIV, but I'm still alive. I've been everywhere in my using days. I've seen all those girls go missing in Vancouver and all that stuff.

Q: You were there during the period of the serial killings?

R: Yeah. I was one of the lucky ones. ▣

Thanh Phuong

The Mind Of A Criminal

and other stories

A True Short Story About My Pet

When I was young, I raised many kinds of chickens. I had many female and only one male — a big rooster. I had him for about seven years. One day I decided I wanted another female, so I sold him to someone down the lane. After that, each morning as soon as my neighbour opened his door he would come running back to my house. I realized how much my rooster missed his home, so my mom gave me the money to buy him back and I never sold him again!

My Memory Is Still There

I'll never forget the years 1978 and 1979. Those years were hungry and many people were without food! Things were very rough and it was hard to survive. Many people committed suicide in those years.

Sometimes I think back to that time. I loved my mom so much. She had to find anything edible to feed us. Sometimes we had only one meal a day, without meat, without vegetables, even without rice. Every day we were so hungry!

I still remember the days my mom had only a couple of bucks. You couldn't buy much. My mom told me to go to buy some fish sauce. After that, my mom took the fish sauce and put it in a small pot to cook it. She stirred and stirred and when the fish sauce became much thicker, she added a little sugar. It turned out a very good sauce. You could eat it with many things. Sometimes we ate like that for a few months.

Sometimes we ate only a few yams for a couple of months. All that time our bodies didn't have much energy. We got tired very easily and we were hungry all the time for a couple of years.

Now that I'm grown up I think of those times and I remember my mom. I love her and I miss her a lot. Her life was so rough, taking care of so many children by herself. I wonder how my mom handled that all those years.

In Vietnam, they called those years the end of the war. My people might call my mom "Widow of our culture."

I Was Lying

When I was a teenager, sometimes I sold a few different kinds of mangoes in front of my house on weekends.

I wanted to make some extra money for "munchies" and for other things I wanted to buy. That was why I sold fruit on weekends.

One time I had only ten bucks (dong) when I went to the market to buy some mangoes to sell in front of my house.

When I arrived at the market, I noticed a group of people gathered around something. I wondered what was going on over there and I kept moving through the group of people until I saw a man lying on the ground who was crying.

The man's leg was badly infected and there was a large hole that went almost right through his muscle.

I could feel his pain! I believe that he was a homeless man.

I felt sorry for him as I stood and looked at him for a while. I took my ten bucks out of my pocket and I said to him, "I only have this much. You take it and buy some meds for your leg."

I went home and sat down in front of my house.

My mom came out of the kitchen and said, "You didn't sell any fruit today, did you?"

I said, "No, Mom, I went to the market, but I lost all of my money."

I still remember the words that my mom shouted: "Oh my God. Are you out of your mind?"

Summer Holiday

Back in Vietnam, a lady came to my house every day. This lady sold lottery tickets to my mom. She was a single mother and she made a lot of money for her family selling the lottery tickets.

One day I decided to tell my mom that I would like to sell lottery tickets. My mother asked me if I could handle it. I said I would try.

The next day my mom went to pick up about 100 lottery tickets. I took the tickets and I went out to sell them the same day. It didn't take long for me to sell them all. I went home and told my mom that I was very happy because I sold all of the tickets so quickly.

A week later, I told my mother I wanted to double the amount of tickets because I was always selling out too quickly. This time my mother took me to the owner of the tickets and asked him to give me credit, as I needed many tickets.

I didn't have to pay the money first. Time went by and I had been selling many tickets every day. I made a lot of money in the next three months.

Then summer holidays ended and I had to go back to school. I gave my mother all of the money I had made. She tapped me on my head with her hand very gently and I was very happy.

That summer holiday I was in grade five. I will never forget it!

The Bench Is Still There

One day during a full moon I went outside for some fresh air. I saw many people walk by me. I kept walking and suddenly I turned my head to the left and saw an Asian girl. Her hair was long, past her shoulders, and the way she walked was so cute! I couldn't hold back and when she walked up beside me I asked her, "Are you Vietnamese?"

She said "Yeah," so I tried to talk to her. When I saw a bench, I asked her, "If you don't mind, could we sit down and talk a little bit?" She said, "No sweat."

She and I sat down and told many different stories about our homeland. I was very excited to hear her stories as I hadn't heard from back home for a long time. A couple of hours later, she said that she had to go and see her mother. I said, "Anyway, thanks for talking to me. Can I see you again sometime?" She said, "I will see you in two days: same place, same time." I went home but my mind was not there. It was on the encounter that I had just had.

Two days later I was there early and I waited for her. A few hours went by, but I didn't see anyone. The street was very quiet and so cold! Just before midnight, I understood that only the bench and I were still there.

Thanh Phuong "Jack" Nguyen was born in Vietnam during the war with the United States. As he describes it, his family, which prospered under the U.S.-dominated regime, suffered hardships after the fall of the Saigon government. With his family's help, Jack immigrated to Canada in search of a better life. He worked hard at a variety of manual labour jobs, including work in a slaughterhouse and as a cook in a fast-food restaurant. He married in Edmonton and became the father of a little girl. He and his wife separated after a few years and Jack moved to Vancouver, where he began seeing the widow of his best friend. At first this new relationship went well, but then it started to go badly. And one winter night after a binge of drinking that had lasted for many days, Jack shot and killed this woman, and shot and killed the woman who had tried to save her. In 1998 Jack was sentenced to life imprisonment.

We visited Jack in Mission Institution on a cool, sunny morning. Mission is located in British Columbia's Fraser Valley. The Institution itself is comprised of a cluster of solid, modern buildings built on rolling, hilly ground. White-tipped mountain peaks loomed in the distance. It had been raining, and although there was morning sun, the sky was filled with grey, rushing clouds.

Jack wore a bright yellow fleece warm-up vest with a white T-shirt and jeans. He was excited, smiling and laughing easily. He spoke English with a very heavy Vietnamese accent. Jack is short and very muscular. He told us he struggles with his weight because of diabetes. Before our interview, Jack accompanied us on a short tour of the Mission Institution grounds. While visiting the chapel, we asked him if Buddhist services, his religion, were held there, and he offered to show us a Buddhist shrine he had in his cell.

Thanh Phuong "Jack" Nguyen's cell can simply be described as beautiful. It seemed he had carefully considered every square inch of his tiny space. Hanging and climbing plants grew around his bed, and the walls were covered with colourful photos, posters, and several intricately detailed paintings of Asian folklore and religious themes. Jack said a now-deceased friend had done the paintings in collaboration with him, though he could not make the precise nature of their collaboration clear to us. Jack also showed us beautiful stylized carvings of birds he had sculpted and painted himself.

On a high shelf in the cell was a simple Buddhist shrine that included an offering of two pears and a photograph of the friend Jack killed. He told us he keeps the shrine so as to think of her, and of his crimes, every day of his life.

Thanh Phuong Nguyen
Born July 5, 1969
Sentenced for second degree murder and manslaughter, 1998
Mission Institution, Mission, British Columbia

INTERVIEW: THANH PHUONG NGUYEN

QUESTION: How did you first come to Canada?

NGUYEN: My mom helped me leave Vietnam by boat. And I'm lucky ... they helped us in the middle of the ocean because my boat was on fire. In the next five minutes if no one helped us … we're all dead. My boat with fifty people, when they took us on the ship, my boat sank right then.

Q: Where did you meet your first wife?

N: In Canada ... in language school. We married and stayed together almost three years.

Q: And the second woman you were with?

N: When I moved to Vancouver I was with my best friend first. But one year later my best friend had an accident and died. … She came to my house every day. Then a year later she fell in love with me, and we lived together.

Q: She had lived with your best friend?

N: My best friend was married to her.

Q: How did he die?

N: My best friend and her went to a wedding and when they came back from the wedding they went to a Vietnamese bar. While they were there, he got stabbed right through the heart. … She was pregnant. At that time she was six months pregnant. Three months later she had a baby. About a year later... I never thought I'd remarry, you know what I mean? But ... it happens in life, right? She'd come to my house every day.

Q: So she was your friend first?

N: Yes. Friend only ... but she was my best friend. [It's a] long story … but we were very happy. I never forget a single day I was with her. I never, never forget all my life. I love her.

Q: And then ... you started drinking?

N: Oh no. I never drank in my whole life. But then ... one day something happened ... December second.

Q: What happened?

N: Her birthday is December second. With us, birthday is not important. All my life I have not [celebrated] even one birthday. But I knew she was born on December second and I try to surprise her for her birthday. Usually every single day I see her in my house. But she didn't show up. I paged her; I called her. Around six o'clock she came down and I asked her where she'd been. I said, "Don't make me worry so much. If I page you, let me know where you are." [It's a] very long story. But something happened and she went home.

Q: You had an argument?

N: Little bit. She slammed the door. [Then] I didn't hear from her. I kept drinking at home. I couldn't eat. About two weeks later I went to a [Buddhist] temple on Granville. At that time I wanted to be a monk; I wanted to stay there for my whole life. But I can't stay there. I go back home. Two weeks later I have a blackout at home. I throw up blood; I think I die. When the cops come to my house I have at least a hundred bottles on the floor. Only one month in my life; I never drink [in] my whole life. And I am there with my gun. I decide to commit suicide. ... I wait for her, I keep drinking. But when I see her, in that second ... if I say I don't remember, maybe call it b.s. I still remember a little bit the moment. I don't know why she ran. ... [Afterwards] I put the gun right up to my head; I pull the trigger; the gun misfires. ... I went to the police department, I put the gun on the table.